Franciscan Studies:
The Difference Women are Making

D1227362

Spirit and Life: A Journal of Contemporary Franciscanism serves as a vehicle for the publication of papers presented at various conferences, symposia, and/or workshops that seek to bring the Franciscan tradition into creative dialogue with contemporary theology, philosophy, psychology, and history. The journal is an occasional publication. During the fiftieth anniversary year of The Franciscan Institute (1991), the publication of this journal was a refounding of an earlier Franciscan Institute Series entitled *Spirit and Life*, established in 1948 by the Reverend Philotheus Boehner, OFM, one of the co-founders and first director of The Franciscan Institute.

The papers contained in this volume were originally presented at Washington Theological Union, Washington, DC, as part of a symposium sponsored by The Franciscan Center, May 29-31, 1998.

Copyright © 1999
The Franciscan Institute
St. Bonaventure University
St. Bonaventure, NY 14778

ISBN 1-57659-164-6

Library of Congress Catalog Card Number:

99-61581

Printed by:
BookMasters
Ashland, Ohio

Spirit and Life

A Journal of Contemporary Franciscanism

Volume 8   *1999*

Franciscan Studies:
The Difference Women are Making

Edited by

Margaret Carney, OSF
Elise Saggau, OSF

Contents

BIOGRAPHICAL INFORMATION

Maria Calisi, PhD, did her doctoral studies in historical theology at Fordham University. Her dissertation was a study of "Bonaventure's Metaphysics of Self-diffusive Goodness and of Exemplarity as a Resource for Feminist Trinitarian Theology." She is now an adjunct professor at St. Peter's College in Jersey City, New Jersey, and at Fordham University. She lives with her husband in the Bronx, New York.

Margaret Carney, OSF, a sister of St. Francis of the Providence of God, Pittsburgh, Pennsylvania, received her doctorate at the Pontificium Athenaeum Antonianum in Rome. Having served as a faculty member at The Franciscan Institute, St. Bonaventure, New York, from 1998-1999, she was appointed Director of the Institute and Dean of the Franciscan Studies program. She is a member of the Franciscan Pilgrimage staff and author of *The First Franciscan Woman, Clare of Assisi & Her Form of Life* (Franciscan Press, 1993). From 1994-96 she chaired the LCWR task force on Leadership Roles for Women in the Church.

Ilia Delio, OSF, a member of the Franciscan Servants of the Holy Child Jesus, North Plainfield, New Jersey, did her doctoral studies in theology at Fordham University. She is presently at Washington Theological Union, Washington, DC, serving as an assistant professor of ecclesial history and Franciscan studies and as Director of the Franciscan Center. She is author of *Crucified Love: Bonaventure's Mysticism of the Crucified Christ* (Quincy: Franciscan Press, 1998).

Paul Lachance, OFM, a friar of the Province of St. Joseph, Montreal, Quebec, is editor and translator of *The Complete Works: Angela of Foligno*, The Classics of Western Spirituality (Paulist Press, 1993). He is an adjunct professor at Chicago Theological Union, teaching courses on Mendicant Spirituality and the Theology of Prayer. He has also taught courses on Franciscan Mystics at the Franciscan Institute, St. Bonaventure University, New York. He has co-translated a dozen books, as well as authored many articles on Franciscan and Christian spirituality, and given numerous retreats, conferences, and workshops in this country, Canada, and abroad. Presently he is working on *Early Franciscan Writings: The Spirituals* for the Classics of Western Spirituality.

Roberta A. McKelvie, OSF, a member of the Bernardine Franciscan Sisters, Reading, Pennsylvania, did her doctoral studies at Fordham University. Her research led her to undertake the task of bringing some Italian sources on Angelina of Montegiove into English so the story of this remarkable woman might be accessible to American Franciscans. She is author of *Retrieving a Living Tradition: Angelina of Montegiove: Franciscan, Tertiary, Beguine* (Franciscan Institute, 1997). She is presently doing historical research for her religious congregation and is an adjunct faculty member at Alvernia College in Reading.

Dominic Monti, OFM, is a friar of Holy Name Province, New York. He received his doctorate from the University of Chicago in 1979, after which he joined the faculty at Washington Theological Union, where he holds the chair in Ecclesiastical History. He specializes in medieval Church history. Among his publications is a translation of *St. Bonaventure's Writings Concerning the Franciscan Order* (Franciscan Institute, 1994).

Elise Saggau, OSF, is a Franciscan Sister of Little Falls, Minnesota. She has a Master of Divinity degree from Loyola University, Chicago, and a Master's degree in Franciscan Studies from the Franciscan Institute. She wrote *A Short History of The Franciscan Federation* (1995). She now serves as assistant director of publications at the Franciscan Institute and is editor of *The Cord.*

Adele Thibaudeau, OSF, a member of the Sisters of St. Francis of Assisi, Milwaukee, Wisconsin, holds a Master's degree in religious studies from Mundelein College, Chicago. She is director of Campus Ministry at Cardinal Stritch University, Milwaukee. Her emphasis in campus ministry is on global awareness, urban immersions, and service learning. She represents her congregation in Franciscan Mission Awareness at Cardinal Stritch University.

Gabriele Ühlein, OSF, is a Franciscan Sister of Wheaton, Illinois, and a member of the national Franciscan Federation Spirit and Life Committee. A Jungian and process theologian, her interdisciplinary doctorate from The Chicago Theological Seminary explored eco-feminist possibilities for both a theological and psychological understanding of the human in a trans-gender species context. She is presently developing the FranCIScan Center for Incarnation Studies in LaPorte, Indiana.

Introduction

The Franciscan Institute is happy to collaborate once again with the Franciscan Center of the Washington Theological Union by the presentation of the proceedings of the 1998 Spring Symposium entitled *Franciscan Studies: The Difference Women Are Making*. A providential design allowed the event to be celebrated on the weekend of Pentecost. Participants thus enjoyed a congruence of liturgy honoring the Spirit unleashed over our still "bent world" and lectures which demonstrated the newness of the voice of women in the field of Franciscan scholarship. The gathering was *Franciscan* in subject matter and style, and so the mutual efforts of women and men were evident throughout the days of formal and familial conversation.

Friar-scholars Dominic Monti, OFM, and Paul Lachance, OFM, offered excellent summaries of the state of Franciscan studies vis-à-vis women's perspectives and women who have singular places in Franciscan history. Ilia Delio, OSF, shared her convictions about the potential of a Franciscan "theology of the good" to ground theological study that harmonizes with women's aspirations. Margaret Carney, OSF, Elise Saggau, OSF, and Roberta Agnes McKelvie, OSF, cooperated to present a historical survey that uncovered multiple factors behind late twentieth-century growth of women scholars in this field. Gabriele Ühlein, OSF, shared her recent research into eco-feminist convictions intersecting with Franciscan tradition and her concerns about Franciscan preferences for preserving the "minor voice" wherever it is heard. Finally, Dr. Maria Calisi unveiled a stimulating approach to knowing and naming the Trinity using Bonaventure's Trinitarian writings as a source for feminist theological reflection.

In addition to hearing speakers whose papers are printed in this volume, the symposium benefited from dialogue with Regis Armstrong, OFM Cap., who has done so much foundational work on the Clare sources, and Dr. Ewert Cousins, who has influenced many students in their choice of Franciscan topics for academic research.

Each break turned into an extended seminar as topics spilled out of the lecture halls and into the many welcoming spaces of the Union building. The loveliness of Washington in late May, the

1

exuberance of the feast of Pentecost, and the energetic exchange of persons in a process that is both personal and professional made for a sojourn that richly repaid each participant's investment.

One sadness shadowed the proceedings. Within the same circle of days, Gedeon Gàl, OFM, one of the most respected Franciscan scholars in the world, was being laid to rest in the cemetery at St. Bonaventure University where he had labored for some thirty years. Mindful of this, we frequently called ourselves to gratitude for those "who have gone before us" in the scholarly pursuit of wisdom. And we reminded ourselves that our accomplishments owe more than we can say to those who have lived hidden lives of laborious work as translators, codicologists, paleographers, editors, and exegetes. We bless their names; we revere their memories.

In such a spirit of thankful awareness, Adele Thibaudeau, OSF, enlivened our proceedings with the composition of a poem in which she invoked the delight in the mind's insatiable hunger for truth and the heart's unending hope for a community in which to sup at wisdom's table. It is with that poetic exclamation that we begin this volume.

Finally, we express our gratitude to Ilia Delio for her gracious coordination of the symposium and assistance to us with this publication, and to Roberta Agnes McKelvie for her editorial advice in the final stages of this project.

Margaret Carney, OSF   The Franciscan Institute
May, 1999

Pentecost Still Happens

Adele Thibaudeau, OSF

We gathered like lionesses
Around a pyrotechtonic fountain: Francis setting fire to our hearts.
A conflagration flowed forth from fraternity: from the Gedeons,
Elises and Margarets, the Robertas and Ewerts, Ingrids, Pauls and
Ilias, the Dominics, Gabrieles and Regises and Marias, and more—
from Bonaventure and Scotus and our beloved Sister Clare.

A melt down moment! Preserve the minor voice!
So long on the fringe, we women in exile began to discover our
power.
Woooooosh!!!! The wind and waves still toss us, turn us, try us!

Gently, personally, profoundly, fraternally, Franciscans all,
the WORD of LOVE flows through us.
"Suddenly our eyes were opened."
We are aflame: The HOLY ONE beside us! The MYSTERY
within us!
And together, sisters and brothers, we know:
HOPE! EMPOWERMENT!

3

Commentary on
"Pentecost Still Happens"

Adele Thibaudeau, OSF

I am exceedingly fascinated by the image of the fountain in St. Bonaventure. He comments on St. Francis's image of God as an overflowing fountain of goodness. In this Pentecost poem, recounting a Franciscan event, I've combined the overflowing fountain image with that of fire. The force of the two images serves to heighten the impact of the power of the event.

In line one, the word "lionesses" is us, and refers to the story offered by Sister Margaret Carney, of the little boy who asked when the lion would win at the book's end. The mother's wise words that only when lions wrote books would the lion win, were an apt opening for this conference on women and higher studies. The further paradox that lions would generally run away from fire may also serve to illustrate the tension and long awaited reality of such a gathering.

In line two, "fraternity" was specifically retained after discussion, interpreted, as Francis did, devoid of its male sexist overtones and pointing to a family bond of equality and inclusiveness. It is very difficult to locate another word with this much weight and meaning for this intent from this tradition. Also the word "pyrotechtonic" was used by Sister Ilia Delio in her description of Francis.

Beginning with line three, I shall simply give the complete names of the many individuals present or referred to who contributed in a specific manner; this was the weekend of the funeral of Father Gedeon Gál, OFM, Hungarian-born philosopher and researcher, author and collaborator at St. Bonaventure's. Others: Sisters Elise Saggau, Margaret Carney, and Roberta McKelvie, Dr. Ewert Cousins, Sister Ingrid Peterson, Father Paul LaChance, Sister Ilia Delio, Father Dominic Monti, Sister Gabriele Uhlein, Father Regis Armstrong, and Maria Calisi.

Sister Gabriele Uhlein used the terms "melt down moment" and "minor" voice in the second stanza.

Beginning with the sound of "Wooosh," we have a reminder of the exquisite Pentecost homily of Father Dominic Monti. With gesture and this rushing sound, he turned to the boat-like hanging sculpture, suspended just to the back of the pulpit, radiating flames. He explained that it symbolized the Church so well for this feast. He spoke of how very personal was the Holy Spirit's presence within each of the faithful and in each of our neighbors, a most feminine image of presence.

Both enhancing and creating the profound experience of the Eucharistic celebration was the music of Michael P. Ward, "In the Breaking of the Bread," as led by a woman cantor with a wondrous voice and accompanied by a Franciscan friar at the piano. The words: "Suddenly our eyes were opened," so powerfully sung repeatedly by the entire assembly, remained a haunting reminder of both the message of the total weekend and the continued transformation that needs to occur if the full flowering of theological studies is to speak a much needed pastoral and healing word, particularly to women of this century.

Roots of the Tradition

Dominic V. Monti, OFM

Where We're Coming From

Just a few days ago, I was telling a former Minister of my province, himself well-versed in Franciscan studies, that I was very much looking forward to participating in a symposium this weekend. When he inquired about the theme, I replied "Franciscan Studies: the Difference Women Are Making." He responded simply: "Considerable!"

Considerable indeed. In fact, I think it fair to say that when future scholars look back on the progress of Franciscan studies in the last quarter of the twentieth century, they will consider the major development to have been the growing prominence of women: both the vastly increased number of women engaged in Franciscan research and the greater recognition given to the women who have shaped our past Franciscan tradition.

The next several days will see a number of talks and a good deal of discussion on this striking development. To introduce us to this topic, I have been asked to explore briefly the roots of this tradition. Doing so, I feel somewhat like the householder in the Gospel parable who brought out from the storehouse things both new and old. On the one hand, we find that this development is a radically new mutation on our Franciscan family tree, but on the other it stretches back to the very base of our roots.

First of all, let us look at the newness—the sea-change which has occurred in just the past two to three decades, as women have sought their rightful access to and recognition in the world of Franciscan studies. As we begin, I believe it is important to recognize just how far we have traveled in the past thirty years. It was only in 1968 that the first wave of what would become a flood tide of feminist thought hit the shores of theological scholarship with the publication of Mary Daly's *The Church and the Second Sex*.[1]

---

[1] Mary Daly, *The Church and the Second Sex* (New York, Harper and Row, 1968).

7

In the intervening years, theologians have been literally overwhelmed with studies which have made it brutally clear that what we regarded as our Catholic "tradition" was shaped almost totally within a male environment. Men controlled the official formulation of Christian doctrine by the Church's hierarchy, its day to day communication through the public preaching of the ordained ministry, and, until very recently, the ongoing teaching of and reflection on that tradition in institutions of higher learning. Indeed, one result of the historical exclusion of women from the shaping of the public tradition of the Christian church is that its theology and practice have suffered from an androcentric and even misogynist basis. Not simply have males been unconsciously assumed to be normative human beings, but women have often been explicitly been defined by the tradition as possessing an inferior humanity.

Nowhere was that male perspective more in evidence in 1968 than in the world of Franciscan studies. Just three years earlier, the latest edition of the standard scholarly biography of St. Francis by Omer Englebert was translated into English by Eve Marie Cooper, with scholarly introductions and notes by Ignatius Brady and Raphael Brown.[2] At the time, the book was hailed as a model of the most current Franciscan scholarship. But just thirty years later, it is shocking to hear Englebert begin his chapter on Clare with the following words:

> A woman is generally worth what the ideas of the man she admires are worth—but her capacity for sacrifice allows her to attain the heights of heroism when that man shows her the way. Thus was with Clare. Who better than anyone else in the world—and almost better than himself—realized the ideal of the Poverello?[3]

We do not know Ms. Cooper's reaction as she translated these words. One might be tempted to say that this was simply Englebert's own prejudice, but then we realize he was merely echoing the view of the previous standard biography, by Johannes Joergensen:

---

[2] Omer Englebert, OFM, *St. Francis of Assisi: A Biography* (Chicago: Franciscan Herald Press, 1965).
[3] Englebert, 160.

While men must sometimes be satisfied to represent theory, practice, often outside all theory—is the vocation of the woman. No one ever realizes more fully a man's ideal than a woman—once she is possessed by it.[4]

Both of these passages are indeed startling to us in 1998, but at least Englebert and Joergensen made their prejudices explicit. For other scholarly treatments of important women in the Franciscan tradition largely shared their beliefs—that women were essentially passive recipients of values and institutional arrangements conceived of and formulated by men.

Women and the Franciscan Educational Conference

These comments about Clare reflect a certain preconception that some historians of the Middle Ages may have had about the role of women, but let us focus for a moment on the impact of women in the world of Franciscan scholarship. One significant barometer here would be the published proceedings of the Franciscan Educational Conference. Organized in 1919 by Thomas Plassmann, OFM, of St. Bonaventure College, its annual meetings probably did the most to retrieve the vast heritage of the Franciscan tradition for the various families of Friars Minor in the United States and Canada. The Conference was a casualty of the immediate post-Conciliar years—brought on by the demise of the minor seminaries, houses of philosophy, and independent theologates of the friars—which incidentally had guaranteed an earlier generation of Franciscan men a solid grounding in the Order's intellectual tradition. In any case, a survey of the contents of the Conference's *Proceedings* over its half-century history provides a fairly accurate reading of the state of Franciscan studies in North America between 1920 and 1970.

In the three decades prior to 1950 there were no contributions to the *Proceedings* by women authors. This in itself is not surprising, given the fact that the Conference was composed only of friar

---

[4]*St. Francis of Assisi: A Biography*, trans. T. O'Connor Sloane (New York: Longmans, Green, and Co., 1912), 122.

participants. But, on the other hand, there are only two references to the topic "woman" or "women" in the index. One of these is a reference to the high standards of classical learning in Western European monasteries of the sixth to the ninth centuries— including those of women. The other is a discussion of "woman" in a lengthy article on "The Asceticism and Mysticism of Fr. Francis of Assisi" by Anthony Linneweber, OFM Speaking of the yearning for the Most High Lord which the Spirit placed in Francis's heart, Linneweber writes:

> The Creator divided the race into two groups—men and women. In the beginning he gave them the command to increase and multiply. Woman is therefore man's mate in giving life to children. . . . Ideal married life is wonderful. . . [but] ideal women are rare. . . .
>
> Francis might have gone in pursuit of such a woman. . . but he gave up the companionship of one ideal woman waiting for him somewhere, only to find Christ waiting for him with open arms. . . . [Too often] men turn to woman for the companionship they ought to seek in Christ and Him alone. The inevitable result is disillusionment. . . . If they could associate with all the women that ever lived, the result would be the same.[5]

I hope I am not wrenching Fr. Linneweber's remarks out of context. He was probably trying to emphasize that some people have been created by God with a longing for the transcendent which calls them to fulfill themselves best in the unique dedication that we call the religious life, but his medieval imagery has made the abstract "woman" a foil—the temptress who embodies the lure of the flesh which would lead his young charges in the seminary from their supernatural goal.

The post-war years did see some small break in the male monopoly of the Franciscan Educational Conference. Congregations of Franciscan sisters committed to the teaching ministry organized their own association in 1953, and at times sisters were invited to present papers at the men's gatherings. All of the contributions

---

[5]*Franciscan Educational Conference: Report of the Annual Meeting*, 8 (1928): 52, 54, 60.

made by women, however, were in specific areas of what were considered female expertise: art, health, educational methods, etc. No women spoke on theological or philosophical topics. For example, at the 1960 meeting of the Conference in Quincy, Illinois, devoted to the theme of "The Family and Franciscan Ideals," several speakers stressed the particular importance of the role of women in the restoration of the place of the family in contemporary society. They emphasized that a woman's primary role should be in the sphere of human relationships, especially the home. In one of the major presentations, the friar author went so far as to state:

> One who has taught women, or even conversed with them, will hardly deny that woman's mind differs from man's. . . . The difference is largely a result of woman's passionality. This passionality limits her intellectual field to the concrete world she lives in and the people around her. . . .
>
> Because she is guided by intuition rather than logical rules, she will not reach the degree of intellectual perfection reached by men. Because intuition is an uneven force, her ideas and conclusions are usually not related or subordinated. Confusion often follows. . . .
>
> It is interesting to note that while woman is capable of very great intellectual achievements—as history and experience proves—intellectual pursuits, scholarly careers, even university education do not interest her. It is much more in accord with her womanliness to be the inspirer of man's work rather than the creator of her own intellectual work. Lombroso significantly says, "The mother of a large family, who has no time to study, . . . has more life, more breadth of ideas than the old maid of the same age who has done nothing else than utter about at universities."[6]

One wonders parenthetically if the author would have also asserted so blithely that a fifty year old man who had raised four children and had built and financed a home had "more breadth of

---

[6]Nicholas Lohkamp, "The Special Importance of Woman's Role in the Restoration of the Family," *Franciscan Educational Conference: Report of the Annual Meeting*, 41 (1960), 199, 201. It should be noted that the author he cites here was a woman, Gina Lombroso.

ideas" than the celibate friar academic, sheltered behind cloister walls? To be balanced, I should mention that he did go on to emphasize the need for contemporary women to be well-educated, but he stressed that

> while many of the subjects young men and women study will be the same, the method, the objectives, and the content of these courses must differ. . . . [For women] there must be a decided bias towards the practical arts and accomplishments called into play in the management of the home.[7]

Within this limited context, the author still made a strong appeal for Franciscan values in the education of women, for

> [its emphasis on] the primacy of love could well direct, enlarge, and exalt woman's need to love. The spontaneous, generous, and altruistic nature of Franciscan action could guide and elevate woman's need to express herself in activity. . . In these and other ways, the Franciscan ideal could be a boon for women. . . This is an area that needs study. The tradition of our Order will reproach us if we turn a deaf ear, and do not respond to this need in true Franciscan style.[8]

As a friar I am embarrassed—and no doubt many women here today are angered—by such cavalier statements; but one point should be underlined in the above argument. True to his announced principles, the friar author presupposes that it is male Franciscans who have the responsibility to unpack for women the intellectual and spiritual tradition of the Order and its contemporary implications for them. This is a task that they cannot do for themselves.

Indeed, it is interesting to note that although a number of Franciscan women did contribute to this volume of papers, all of them focused on specialized themes which reflected traditional women's roles in the fields of health care and education: "The

---

[7]Lohkamp, 221-22.
[8]Lohkamp, 222.

Family and Its Aging Members," "Teaching Christian Family Living," "Home-Hospital Relations," and "Health for the Family." Clearly, very few women at the time had any role in Franciscan studies as we are using the term in this conference. One can also illustrate this statement by examining the first thirty volumes (1941-70) of the premier English-language journal, *Franciscan Studies*. Over these three decades only six women can be found among the two hundred scholars who contributed articles.[9]

A Breakthrough at The Franciscan Institute

Most of these few exceptions among American women who had broken the male monopoly to make a contribution to the world of Franciscan studies—as we will hear from Margaret Carney—had been nourished by Philotheus Boehner, OFM, and Thomas Plassmann, OFM, at the Franciscan Institute of St. Bonaventure University. One of these, Emma Therese Healy, SSJ, completed her dissertation on Bonaventure's *De reductione artium ad theologiam*, which became the first book written under the auspices of the newly founded Franciscan Institute. At Fr. Philotheus's urging, she later embarked on a much more detailed study, *Woman According to St. Bonaventure*, which was published in 1956. Although Healy was still working within the constraining categories of the dominant neo-Scholastic philosophy of the times, her work was a groundbreaking study. In the preface she noted:

> Since the gates of Paradise lost clanged behind her and her hapless spouse, Woman has been the most controversial figure in the history of the world—the perennial theme of poets, philosophers, and theologians. To some she is an angel in the flesh, to others, the only mistake God ever made.[10]

Is it too much to see here a plea from a woman to male philosophers and theologians to be taken seriously as an equal—both

---

[9]I did not count the authors of book reviews, but only of the major articles. (Editor's note: For more information on the Franciscan Educational Conference see Margaret Carney's article in this volume, pp. 94-6.)

[10]Emma Therese Healy, *Woman According to St. Bonaventure* (New York: Georgian Press, 1956), v.

as a human being and as a scholar—neither the delicate figurine on a pedestal or the "gates of hell" temptress, traces of which are evident in the two papers we have examined above?

Rather, Healy's study had led her to a telling conclusion— "actually, the status of women in any age is a concrete expression of the philosophy which dominate the age in which she lives."[11] Her study of St. Bonaventure made her realize that his perceptions of women, intellectually and spiritually, were the products of a certain culture. The abstract idea of "woman" assumed by the Franciscan authors we have examined was in reality a social construct—largely the perception of men—not the distillation of some eternal truth. Interestingly enough, this idea was also pointed out several years later in a response to Lohkamp's paper at the 1960 Franciscan Educational Conference which I cited extensively earlier. This speaker—also a friar—wondered:

> How many and how much of the normative propositions we reach in our philosophy are natural absolutes as opposed to culturally-evolved directives or conventions of society? If the working mother is here to stay, as some sociologists and psychologists insist, who are we to put up a sign "Not allowed beyond this point"? Perhaps it is best to sum up by expressing a hope that the rapidly rising educational levels of sisters' congregations will prompt development in detail on the question of 'woman.' . . . Only then can we propose a solid doctrine on the education of woman as woman.[12]

Emergence of New Consciousness

These remarks were truly prophetic. In the later 1960s, more and more women gained access to the academic tools and the public forum of teaching and research. Spurred on by the growing interest in social history, they initiated a more systematic inquiry into the Christian tradition from a woman's perspective, thus exposing its androcentric and even mysoginist biases. The results of the last quarter century of such research has enabled us to see what we now call "gender issues." We have come to realize that "to be born a

---

[11]Healy, v.
[12]Response by Marcian Schneider, *Franciscan Educational Conference: Report of the Annual Meeting*, 41 (1960), 229.

man or a woman in any society is more than a simple biological fact. It is a biological fact with social implications." We realize now that all cultures "reformulate what begins as a fact of nature—sexual differentiation—redefining, representing, and valuing it, channeling men and women into different roles, relationships, and institutions."[13]

All of this is still quite *new* in the world of Franciscan studies. Thirty years ago, we never could have had a symposium like this—at least outside of a small seminar room which might have held the few women engaged in Franciscan research at the time. But at the same time, this new presence of women scholars has led to a rediscovery of something which in fact is very *old*—the absolutely essential role of women in the growth and development of the Franciscan tradition.

The rise of a feminist social and historical criticism has launched a thoroughgoing interrogation of our Christian and Franciscan past. And so over the last three decades, we have witnessed an ever-increasing concern to reclaim the lost history of women, to let their suppressed voices finally be heard. There has been a commitment to unmask the history that has been written solely from the perspective of its male participants. Thus we have been led to a radically changed perspective on the women in our Franciscan tradition, and thus the character and direction of the whole Franciscan movement has been radically changed as well.

Women: Silent and Invisible

This is difficult work. Trying to evaluate the surviving extant records which contain the voices of early Franciscan women is a tedious task. Those who search them must learn to be alert, patient, and sensitive listeners. Why is this the case? The titles of two recent works illustrate the problems for contemporaries who would try to embark on this task. Christine Klapisch-Zuber, who edited the second volume of the recent *History of Women*, entitled it *The Silences of the Middle Ages*;[14] and an insightful essay, especially

---

[13]Christine Klapish-Zuber, "Including Women," trans. Arthur Goldhammer, in *A History of Women*, Vol. 2, *The Silences of the Middle Ages* (Cambridge: The Belkap Press, 1992), 3. (Paraphrased slightly.)
[14]See note 13.

valuable for those who would study the context of the first Franciscan women, is called "Invisible Madonnas? The Italian Historiographical Tradition and the Women of Medieval Italy."[15] How do contemporary students reach these women, when the historical sources we possess often made them "silent" and "invisible"? We have to face the fact that the most prominent voices and figures in our medieval sources are male—for men enjoyed the legal autonomy and the right to speak publicly that were either denied women or granted only grudgingly.

Christine de Pisan, a "feminist" of the early fifteenth century, tells us that for some time she lamented the misfortune of being born a woman, until she came to see that her miserable condition was due to a "series of male authorities." The abstract "woman" after all was a creation of male minds who had molded the dominant philosophy and theology of the times and the institutions which embodied them. That is why the first article in Klapish-Zuber's volume is entitled "The Clerical Gaze"—for in the Middle Ages virtually all of these men were clergy.[16] They controlled the written word, the flow of knowledge, through both pulpits and academic teaching positions, which determined how people conceived of "woman." This image created the context in which most writers of the time—also clerics—described the individual women they encountered.

The supposed superiority of men over women was based firmly in ancient science, formulated by Aristotle in the fourth century B.C. Within his framework, the physical universe was constituted of matter and form. In regards to the formation of human beings, women constituted matter, chaotic and formless, while men provided the life-giving principle of form. As matter deprived of form, the female was an imperfect and incomplete version of the male, related to the opposite sex as mere receiver and inferior instrument. Women had also inherited an unhealthy combination of the four physical elements which combined to form the bodily humors. Women were, consequently, dominated by melancholic

---

[15]Diane Owen Hughes, "Invisible Madonnas? The Italian Historiographical Tradition and the Women of Medieval Italy, in *Women in Medieval History and Historiography*, ed. Susan Mosher Stuard (Philadelphia: University of Pennsylvania Press, 1987), 25-57.

[16]Jacques Delarun, "The Clerical Gaze," trans. Arthur Goldhammer, in Klapish-Zuber, 15-42. The Christine de Pisan reference is on p. 1 of the same work.

humors—which predisposed them to moodiness and depression and what today we would call neurotic behavior. This view of females as defective, not fully rational males provided a scientific basis for medieval society's subjection of women to men, and hence determined the hierarchy of male over female in all aspects of medieval life.[17]

But the dominant view of woman was based only in part on this biological argument. More crucial to the Church's position regarding the natural inferiority of women in society was the female role in the Genesis story of the creation of humankind and its fall from grace. This narrative asserted man's primacy over woman, who was created after man and from one of his ribs in order to give him a "helper"—interpreted by most medieval theologians as a helper necessary for the work of generating new human beings. Perhaps even more important was that Eve, after being seduced by the serpent, persuaded Adam to join her in disobedience to God's will. In this she bore the brunt of the divine curse: she would henceforth bring forth her children in pain and be dominated by her husband. Clerical teachers, instructing their adolescent clerical charges at the height of their sexual drives, naturally dwelt on this feature of women as embodying "fallen" human nature, a constant intoxicating threat to the moral and spiritual purity of men.

Such opinions formed the mental outlook Franciscan friars brought to their sisters and naturally colored the accounts they would write of them. How could a woman's authentic voice be filtered through the stereotypes often imposed—even unintentionally—by a male narrator? A woman had tremendous handicaps—both natural and religious—to overcome in order to assert any claim to charismatic spiritual leadership or to contribute to the realm of abstract thought.

Furthermore, medieval Italian records, so crucial for understanding the first generation of the Franciscan movement, render women even more "silent" and "invisible" than those of Northern Europe. The abundant historical documents of the urban communes where the Franciscan movement originated scrutinize women much less thoroughly than they do men. First of all, Italian feudal law placed a woman under a permanent wardship, either that

---

[17]Claude Thomasset, "The Nature of Woman," in Klapish-Zuber, 43-69.

of her father or her husband. Many Italian communes required that any woman entering a contract must first obtain the express approval of a male relative; furthermore, the republican form of government under which the communes lived restricted the role of the hereditary nobility in which women did exercise some influence and even office through their family connections. Finally, Italy, like other Mediterranean lands, nurtured a strong cultural prejudice against female participation in all forms of public life. Virtuous maidens, especially past the age of puberty, were expected to limit their contacts with the world beyond the household. In short, men and women in medieval towns operated in widely separate spheres. Men held a virtual monopoly over public office; women, on the other hand, presided over the daily activities that were centered in the household routine. Only a few women resisted the cloistering impulses of family and Church. In the extant records few speak in their own voice.[18]

Needless to say, women were excluded from higher education— especially once university regulations were codified in the thirteenth century—even though large numbers of middle and upper class girls received a grammar school education in medieval towns. Thus they never gained the professional expertise to become masters of the Franciscan philosophical and theological tradition in an academic sense.

New Voices; New Visibility

But despite these difficulties, our early Franciscan sisters are finally beginning to regain both visibility and a voice, taking their rightful place as important subjects of Franciscan study today. We have made great efforts to overcome the obstacles inherent in the medieval sources and are learning to "read past" the preconceptions of the typical male narrator. We are able to peer between the lines to see the real women contained in the text, giving our attention to what medieval women were actually saying about their religious experience and about life among their sisters. We are finally starting to gain a better appreciation of these early Franciscan women for themselves.

---

[18]Cf. Hughes, "Invisible Madonnas."

Authors like Carolyn Bynum have begun to unpack the richness of the religious expression of medieval women. Their behavior shows that they generally did not internalize the misogynist attitudes of the dominant culture as we might expect. In fact,

> religious women paid surprisingly little attention to their supposed incapacity. Although told by the theological tradition that qua women, they were not created fully in God's image, women writers ignored the warning.[19]

Indeed, medieval Franciscan women did not view themselves as "woman," but asserted and embraced their full humanity. This makes them apt subjects of study for Franciscan theology and spirituality today. After all, Franciscanism is not an abstract ideology but a life according to the Gospel—a decisive experience of God which leads men and women to view other human beings and their world differently. Theology is simply an attempt to communicate that experience in words, and academic theologians are not the only ones—or perhaps not even the best ones—to do that.

Today, we are grateful for the collaborative effort of women and men Franciscan scholars who have given our medieval sisters an increased visibility and captured their authentic voices: Regis Armstrong, Margaret Carney, and Ingrid Peterson for Clare of Assisi; Paul Lachance for Angela of Foligno; Roberta McKelvie for Angelina of Montegiove, to name a few.[20] For the rest of this conference, we will discuss treasures new and old. We will attend to the newness of women scholars in the field of Franciscan studies, who are framing unconventional perspectives and asking previously unformulated questions. We will rediscover Franciscan women from the past, too long silent, misunderstood, or marginalized, and now

---

[19]Carolyn Walker Bynum, ". . . 'And Women His Humanity'": Female Imagery in the Religious Writing of the Later Middle Ages," in *Gender and Religion: On the Complexity of Symbols*, ed. C. W. Bynum, S. Harrell, and P. Richman (Boston: Beacon Press, 1986), 260.

[20]See Regis Armstrong, *Clare of Assisi: Early Documents*, revised edition (St. Bonaventure, NY: The Franciscan Institute, 1993); Margaret Carney, *The First Franciscan Woman* (Quincy, IL: Franciscan Press, 1993); Ingrid Peterson, *Clare of Assisi: A Biographical Study* (Quincy, IL: Franciscan Press, 1998); Paul Lachance, *Angela of Foligno: The Complete Works* (New York: Paulist Press, 1998); Roberta McKelvie, *Retrieving a Living Tradition: Angelina of Montegiove* (St. Bonaventure, NY: The Franciscan Institute, 1997).

brought to the forefront of scholarly and popular consciousness. It is a vibrant time.

The first Franciscan century witnessed the energy of a fresh evangelical vision which radically transformed the lives of both women and men. Perhaps the difference women are making in Franciscan studies today can help their contemporary brothers and sisters re-found a life according to the Gospels in a new millennium.

The Renaissance of Franciscan Theology:
Retrieving the Tradition of the Good

Ilia Delio, OSF

Introduction

When I first proposed a conference on the impact of women in Franciscan studies, I found the idea exciting. However, several of our young student friars thought the idea was a waste of time. As one said: "Women in Franciscan studies? The whole thing should be over in fifteen minutes!" I think this young man's response sums up a general feeling—what do women have to offer to Franciscan studies and, in particular, to Franciscan theology? I could be flippant and say, "everything," but I would like to spell this out more clearly.

The term "Franciscan theology" is very complex if one considers the tradition in its entirety. My use of the term, however, identifies a particular set of relations between God, humanity, and the world that arose out of the religious experience of Francis and crystallized in the theology of Bonaventure and Duns Scotus. I maintain that *Franciscan* theology developed in the thirteenth century, culminated in the fourteenth century, and dissipated afterwards. Theology was authentically Franciscan in the Middle Ages because it was grounded in the self-diffusive good or love of God. Francis himself, in many of his prayers, referred to God as the supreme good, the all good, the most high good.[1] To speak of the good is to speak of the fountain fullness of God's love. This is the essential meaning of the incarnation for Franciscans—that God who is love is totally expressed in the life, death, and resurrection of Jesus Christ. This realization of divine love in the world in Christ ushers in a new system of relations characterized by mutuality, compassion, and *fraternitas*—themes that can be identified in Francis's writings, in the *legendae*, and which are distilled theologically by Bonaventure and Scotus.

---

[1] See, for example, Francis's "Praises To Be Said at All the Hours," where he proclaims: "All-powerful, most holy, most high, and supreme God: all good, supreme good, totally good, You who alone are good; may we give You all praise, all glory, all thanks, all honor, all blessing, and all good things. So be it. So be it. Amen." Engl. trans. Regis Armstrong, OFM Cap. and Ignatius Brady, OFM, *Francis and Clare: The Complete Works* (New York: Paulist, 1982), 102.

Franciscan theology, springing up from the experience of Francis, espouses ideals similar to feminist theology today with an emphasis on mutual relationships, integration, and a holistic view of created reality.[2] It is my thesis that authentic Franciscan theology, rooted in the good, embodies the principles of contemporary feminist theology, that is, Franciscan theology is essentially feminist in principle. And it is precisely on this note that I believe the inclusion of women in Franciscan theology today is not simply commendable but vital.

From the beginning of the tradition, women were part of the theological enterprise insofar as their personal experience of God led them to articulate an understanding of God in relation to humanity and the created world. Margaret Carney claims that at some point in the tradition, the mystical pedagogy of women mystics influenced the formal theology of the friars.[3] While women mystics maintained an authentic Franciscan tradition of the good even under the most adverse circumstances, their voices in theology were ultimately suppressed. In the tradition-at-large, theology developed as a male endeavor from the late Middle Ages up to the twentieth century. While theology developed, it also departed from the tradition of the good, becoming a theology based on being and a melange of philosophical ideas. Heavily intellectual and Thomistic in form, Franciscan theology became the privilege of a few, divorced from daily Christian life.

The rebirth of Franciscan theology within the last fifty years has been accompanied by the inclusion of women. These events are not merely coincidental but rather symbiotic. The admission of women to Franciscan studies has and continues to change the nature of theology itself, and this change corresponds to the rebirth of Franciscan theology as a feminist liberating theology. The attraction of women to the good, that is, to a theology that ensures mutually affirming relationships, is at the heart of the renewal of Franciscan theology.

In order to examine the renaissance or rebirth of Franciscan theology, I have divided the presentation into five parts: the first part

---

[2]According to Alfonso Pompei the "Franciscanism" of the theology is accurately described by a list of predicates. It is personal/relational, practical and affective, pregnant and contemplative, voluntaristic and psychological, biblical/historical/salvific. Franciscan theology evolves, he states, just so that it may remain truly, and not merely ideologically, Franciscan. See Alfonso Pompei, "The *Sermones* of St. Anthony and Franciscan Theology," trans. Edward Hagman, *Greyfriars Review* 9:3 (1995): 301.

[3]See Margaret Carney, OSF, "Franciscan Women and the Theological Enterprise," in *The History of Franciscan Theology*, ed. Kenan B. Osborne, OFM (St. Bonaventure, NY: The Franciscan Institute, 1994), 333-6.

identifies terms that we frequently encounter but seldom fully understand. Hopefully, these brief definitions will provide a clearer meaning to the renewal of Franciscan theology. The second part examines the characteristics of feminist theology in order to draw a comparison to Franciscan theology. Thirdly, I examine Franciscan theology as a theology of the good, arising out of the experience of Francis and developing in Bonaventure. The fourth part looks at the Franciscan women mystics—Clare of Assisi, Veronica Giuliani, and Angela of Foligno—as early Franciscan women theologians. The fifth part discusses the task of women today in Franciscan theology as the task of retrieving the good. I will conclude with some thoughts on Franciscan theology in light of the Church of the new millennium.

I. Definition of Terms

In order to elucidate the task of women in Franciscan theology, I would like to define some terms that we frequently encounter, namely, "theology," "spirituality," and "praxis." Theology is commonly defined as a disciplined reflection on faith which seeks to express the contents of faith in clear and coherent language. In its most literal sense, theology means "God-talk." Karl Rahner defines theology as the science of faith. It seeks to know God and the things of God and to direct human beings to God, their ultimate end. The question of interest is: what is the starting point of theology? Does it begin with Scripture and tradition or with personal experience? From the Council of Trent up to Vatican II, theology was almost exclusively based on Scripture and revelation in an attempt to formulate propositional truths about the faith. Theology of this type was viewed "from above." Post Vatican II developments in theology have led to an emphasis on personal experience as the starting point of theology. We see this primarily in liberation theologies, for example, feminist theology. Since the starting point of theology is from experience, theology is viewed "from below." Franciscan theology, although arising in the Middle Ages, is essentially a theology from below because it is rooted in personal experience.

In the Middle Ages Franciscan theology was not distinguished from spirituality but rather was seen as knowledge for the sake of a deepening love. Today, however, spirituality is acknowledged as a discipline in its own right, although scholars have difficulty in defining exactly what spirituality is and how it relates to theology. Walter Principe claims that spirituality points to those aspects of a person's living faith or commitment that concern his or her striving to attain the highest ideal or goal.[4] Jordan Aumann states that spirituality refers to any religious or ethical value that is concretized as an attitude or spirit from which one's actions flow.[5] Pierre Pourrat indicates that spirituality is that *part* of theology that deals with Christian perfection and the ways that lead to it.[6] Pourrat's rather narrow definition highlights some of the tension between spirituality and theology. Is spirituality a *part* of theology or is it independent of theology? Or are they one and the same? In order to resolve this tension, the term *praxis* is helpful. Praxis refers to theological reflection and informed action. That is, the way one thinks about God informs or determines one's actions in the world. Praxis, in a sense, unites theology and spirituality. Liberation theologies today espouse theology as praxis. Feminist theology, in particular, focuses on knowledge of God that informs actions of mutual relationship as well as actions that seek to eradicate oppressive relationships due to domination and power.

Ideally, Franciscan theology, like feminist theology, is a theology of praxis. Knowledge of God is meant to transform the person into communion with God and neighbor. That which marked the theology of early Franciscan theologians like Bonaventure and Scotus was the fact that theology's goal was not simply a way of doing or knowing, but rather of being human in the image of the divine trinitarian mystery of personhood and communion. Being human in a particular way meant being united with God and one another in a communion of love as an imitation of the love which Christ embodied.[7]

Both Franciscan theology and feminist theology are, ideally, oriented toward personhood and communion. In both, theological reflection is to lead one into personal relationship with God and neighbor for the sake of a deeper and fuller life. In the early phase of the tradition, what characterized Franciscan theology as a dynamic theology was that it arose out of personal experience and, ultimately,

---

[4]Walter Principe, "Toward Defining Spirituality," *Studies in Religion* 12 (1983): 139.

[5]See Bernard McGinn, "The Letter and the Spirit: Spirituality as an Academic Discipline," *Christian Spirituality Bulletin*, 1.2 (Fall, 1993): 5.

[6]McGinn, 4.

[7]Mary Elizabeth Ingham, "John Duns Scotus: An Integrated Vision," in *The History of Franciscan Theology*, 227.

was meant to transform that experience. Franciscan theology, from the beginning, demanded praxis. What history has handed down to us, however, is an intellectual theological tradition that has had little impact on our daily lives. This loss corresponds historically to the exclusion of women from the whole theological endeavor. The retrieval of an authentic Franciscan theology today corresponds to the inclusion of women in the theological enterprise, and the participation of women is helping to redefine Franciscan theology as one that is feminist and liberating in principle.

II. Aspects of Feminist Theology

In her introduction to the book, *Freeing Theology*, the late Catherine LaCugna states that the presence of women theologians not only has changed the sociology of who is doing theology today but it has fundamentally changed the way of doing theology.[8] I believe this is an important statement for us as we begin to examine the impact of women on Franciscan theology. It is not simply the fact that women are *doing* theology but the fact that *women* are doing Franciscan theology that is changing the nature of the theology itself. The changing nature of Franciscan theology is made clearer in light of feminist theology.

Feminist theology takes as its starting point the experience of women. It denounces whatever is dehumanizing to women and announces the transformation of society.[9] A fundamental principle of feminism is that both women and men share fully in human nature and that neither is superior to the other. Theological feminism draws its strength of conviction from women whose experience tells them that the kingdom of God preached by Jesus promises a different order of relationships among persons than the one that prevails today. Regina Coll identifies the characteristics of feminist theology as: 1) praxis-centered, 2) comprehensive, 3) holistic, and 4) consciously ideological.[10] Feminist theology, as a theology of reflection and action, focuses on the liberation of women and men from the oppressive burden of patriarchy. It is an inclusive type of theology that emphasizes mutual relationships

---

[8]*Freeing Theology: The Essentials of Theology in Feminist Perspective*, ed. Catherine Mowry LaCugna (New York: HarperCollins, 1993), 2.

[9]Regina A. Coll, *Christianity and Feminism in Conversation* (Mystic, CT: Twenty-Third Publ., 1994), 12.

[10]Coll, 14-6.

not only between men and women but also between humanity and the non-human created world. The long range hope, according to Coll, is that feminist theology, like all liberation theologies, will become obsolete as a sub-discipline because it will so affect theological thought that all theologies will be colored by the principles of feminism and will draw from the reflection of the lives of women and men.[11]

Outstanding contributions by women have been made in the effort to articulate a comprehensive feminist theology. These include studies in systematic theology, biblical theology, and spirituality. Important works by Elizabeth Johnson and Catherine LaCugna, for example, have helped reshaped Christian thinking by retrieving God from a patriarchy based on ontological difference to a God who is by nature a community of relationships.[12] Feminist theology raises the point that if God is truly the ground of our lives and our world, then the way we view God influences the way we live in the world. This point is equally essential to Franciscan theology. In this respect, LaCugna's work on the Trinity helps us to identify a feminist theology of God that resonates with Franciscan theology. Her work sheds light on locating the roots of feminist theology in Franciscan theology primarily because she highlights the essence of God as relational, rooted in the good.

LaCugna distinguishes between the Latin model of the Trinity and the Greek model. The Latin model, derived from Augustine's notion of divine persons and the nature of God as one substance, led to an emphasis on God not as persons but as Being. Thomas Aquinas referred to the Trinity as Being in act. God is the pure act of being.[13] Thomas's model upholds a tradition of being where being is prior to personhood. What one is in oneself is prior to who one is in relation to another. This notion of God as perfect absolute being corresponds to patriarchy as the rule of the father; it leads also to autonomy, nondetermination by another, and self-possession as prior to self-gift. The Greek model of the Trinity (which Bonaventure followed) posits relatedness as the supreme characteristic of God. It does not view God essentially as being but as good, and the nature of the good (the highest good being love) is

---

[11]Coll, 14.

[12]See Elizabeth A. Johnson, *Consider Jesus: Waves of Renewal in Christology* (New York: Crossroad, 1990), 93 and *She Who Is: The Mystery of God in Feminist Theological Discourse* (New York: Crossroad, 1996), 150-245; Catherine Mowry LaCugna, *God For Us: The Trinity and Christian Life* (San Francisco: Harper San Francisco, 1991).

[13]Catherine Mowry LaCugna, "God in Communion With Us," in *Freeing Theology,* 89.

to share itself with another. Thus, God is by nature outgoing love and self-gift.[14] The nature of God is to give God's self away, to be in relationship with another. In this way, all existence is derived from an absolutely personal principle, the diffusive love of God.

The destiny of the human person is to live in authentic communion with God, with other persons, and with all God's creatures.[15] In the tradition of the good, the model of the Trinity based on the self-diffusive good means true communion is the deepest meaning of life and arises out of a genuine diversity among equals. LaCugna suggests that by the Middle Ages both Greek and Latin models of the Trinity were obsolete. The Trinity itself, she states, became a kind of monad in the Christian life, a type of self-sufficient divine community. Christianity found itself in the strange position of having a trinitarian doctrine of God on the books, but in practice its theology had become unitarian.[16]

While LaCugna's argument is appealing, it is really not borne out in the Franciscan tradition, at least in its early phase. I would argue that the charism of Francis of Assisi, theologically formulated by Bonaventure, returned the Trinity to the vital center of the Christian life and in doing so gave way to a theology of mutual relationships that could be described as feminist. It is Bonaventure who resurrects the Greek model of the Trinity, ushering in a new ground of existence through the tradition of the good or love as the ground of all reality.[17] I would like to turn now to examine more closely the emergence of theology in the Franciscan tradition and to see how its beginning was truly life-giving for the church.

III. Relation of Feminist Theology to Franciscan Theology

Zachary Hayes states that if anything can be said about Francis of Assisi, it is that he was a man of profound, even radical, religious experience. Perhaps Francis's greatest bequest to later generations is a vision of human life and an insight into the meaning of the gospel that

---

[14]"God in Communion With Us," 87-9.
[15]"God in Communion With Us," 98, 92.
[16]"God in Communion With Us," 90.
[17]I *Sent.* d. 27, p. 1, a.u., q. 2, ad 3 (I, 471).

demands serious reflected thought.[18] The writings we have from Francis indicate that he had deep theological insights. Although Francis was not a trained theologian, hardly even literate, he was, as Bernard McGinn suggests, a vernacular theologian.[19] Theology sprang up from his own experience of God, and he articulated this experience in his Umbrian dialect.

The life of Francis is well known, with his desire to follow the poor Christ, to live radical poverty, and to preach the Gospel. While his charism is both Christ-centered and Trinity-centered, perhaps the single most significant aspect of his life was his relationship to Jesus Christ. This intimate relationship formed the basis of his intense spiritual life, his growing into a deeper relationship with God, with his neighbor, and with the non-human created world. Through his union with Christ, Francis came to realize relationships of mutuality with all of creation. From the marginalized leper to the tiniest earthworm, Francis saw himself as brother to all, just as God had become intimately united to all in the incarnation of the Word.

Bonaventure describes Francis as a truly pious person, that is, intimately related to God, neighbor, and creation.[20] The basis of this piety, Bonaventure states, is the spirit of compassionate love that Francis developed through his conformity to Christ. This spirit of compassionate or self-giving love enabled Francis to be self-giving in his relationships. Through his union with Christ Francis came to realize that all created things—the sun, the moon, the stars—are his brothers and sisters, because all are intimately related to Christ, the Word of God. His final song of praise is the *Canticle of Brother Sun*.

It would not be inappropriate to suggest that Francis's theology is one of the first in the Christian tradition to challenge the notion of God as perfect, self-sufficient being insofar as he affirmed God as dynamic, self-diffusive goodness. By focusing on the incarnation as the manifestation of God's love in the world, Francis perceived that God is

---

[18]Zachary Hayes, OFM, "Franciscan Tradition as Wisdom Tradition," in *Franciscan Leadership in Ministry: Foundations in History, Theology, and Spirituality*, Spirit and Life Series, 7 (St. Bonaventure, NY: The Franciscan Institute, 1997), 30.

[19]Bernard McGinn, "Was Francis of Assisi a Mystic?" in *Doors of Understanding: Conversations on Global Spirituality in Honor of Ewert Cousins*, ed. Steven L. Chase (Quincy, IL: Franciscan Press, 1997), 148.

[20]Bonaventure, "The Life of St. Francis," 8:1, in *Bonaventure*, trans. Cousins, 250.

to be found *in* the world.[21] Bonaventure would later say that, in the incarnation, God humbly bent down to take our human nature into unity with the divine nature; thus, *all of creation* reflects the "footprints of God."[22] In this way, the spiritual journey is not about leaving the world to go to God but discovering God in the world through Jesus Christ.

While Francis ushers in a new way of perceiving God in the world, it is Bonaventure, the theologian and minister general, who crystallizes Francis's charism into a theological world view. As a trained theologian, Bonaventure articulates the meaning of theology as praxis, the purpose of which is to lead one to God, the ultimate good. For Bonaventure, theology in its intellectual dimensions is an important discipline, but it cannot be allowed to be limited to the intellectual level. Theology is practical in the sense that it contributes to the intellectual, moral, and spiritual transformation of the human being. It should ultimately flow into a transformed style of life. The theological endeavor as intellectual is to lead the human person to affective contemplative delight in the good and beautiful.[23] For Bonaventure, knowledge is bound up with love, and this love must express itself in personal action. Theology and spirituality, therefore, are intertwined.

As for Francis, the single most important aspect of "God-talk" for Bonaventure is the incarnation and, more specifically, the Crucified Christ. Reflecting on the meaning of Christ Crucified in the life of Francis, Bonaventure realized that "there is no other path [to God] but through the burning love of the Crucified."[24] For Bonaventure, as for Francis, Christ Crucified is not about a male Savior who saves sinful humanity. Rather, the Crucified is about the fullness of divine love in the world. The overflowing fountain of God's love is expressed in the wounds of Jesus on the cross.

Bonaventure described the spirit of love manifested in Christ as compassionate love—love that goes out to the other and unites with the

---

[21]As Hayes states, "The spiritual journey is deeply embedded in the cosmos itself." See Zachary Hayes, "Christology—Cosmology" *Franciscan Leadership in Ministry*, 57.

[22]Bonaventure, "Sermon II On the Nativity of the Lord," in *What Manner of Man? Sermons on Christ by St. Bonaventure*, trans. Zachary Hayes (Chicago: Franciscan Herald Press, 1989), 57.

[23]Hayes, "Franciscan Tradition as Wisdom Tradition," 35-6.

[24]Bonaventure, "The Soul's Journey into God," Prol. 3, in *Bonaventure, The Soul's Journey into God, The Tree of Life, The Life of St. Francis*, trans. Ewert Cousins (New York: Paulist Press, 1978), 54.

other for the sake of a deeper and fuller life. He described Christ Crucified as the wisdom of God, that is, the love of God that brings about order and peace in the world. Bonaventure came to realize that Francis was truly a man of peace who lived in right relationship with his neighbor and with creation. He had learned to love in the way that God loves. This type of love, bound up with poverty and humility, is a love that holds back nothing for itself but gives itself away entirely just as God has given God's self totally to us in the incarnation of the Word.

For Bonaventure, the diffusion of divine love in the cosmos through the incarnation established a new way of thinking about God and the world. God is not a perfect absolute being who creates a hierarchy of beings nor a self-sufficient substance with personhood added on. Rather, God is an overflowing fountain of love who, by the very nature of God as love, gives God's self away. For Bonaventure, as for Francis, *that* God is is secondary to *who* God is. If God were not personal love, God would not exist at all. The notion of God as self-diffusive good or essential love led to a new view of the incarnation. Bonaventure interpreted the incarnation as an event not primarily about sin, but about the love of God. The incarnation is about the supreme gift of God who is love given to us in the person of Jesus Christ. It signifies that all of creation is essentially "loved" into being.

Understanding the Trinity as a communion of love enabled Bonaventure to understand Francis's life in a deeper way. He interpreted Francis's life as a growth in personhood and communion with God, neighbor, and creation. Francis grew in his love for neighbor and the lowly creatures of creation because he came to recognize them as family, sharing the same source of reality as himself, that is, the overflowing love of God. In this way, he was led to a deeper spirit of compassionate love that sought to give itself away, to be in union with the other. It is no secret that Francis desired martyrdom because he saw this perfect path of love as one of total self-gift, following the example of Jesus Christ. In light of Francis, Bonaventure understands that totally self-giving love entails suffering because it seeks nothing for itself but rather desires to give itself completely to the other. Only one conformed to Christ Crucified can attain the level of love which brings about unity with one's neighbor and all of creation.

By grounding all existence in the self-diffusive good or love of God, Bonaventure transformed the God of hierarchy based on being into a

God of communion of persons based on love. He saw that God's love, poured out in the life of Jesus Christ, ushered in a new system of relationships based on the good. Using contemporary language, we can describe these relationships in several ways:

1) They are non-hierarchical. Because the Trinity is a community of love and that love is embodied in Christ and because each person is made in the image of Christ, no one person is superior in dignity to another; rather, all are equal.

2) They are non-dualistic. The soul is not superior to the body; rather the body shares the nobility of the soul. Thus, the body is not brute matter but, together with the soul, makes the journey to God.

3) They are mutually affirming. Reflecting on Francis's life, Bonaventure teaches that relationships are not pragmatic but are a sharing with the other for the sake of a deeper and fuller life.

4) They are holistic. The journey to God is not exclusive to the human person but includes the non-human created world as well. The destiny of the cosmos is intertwined with the human journey. Material reality is sacramental for Bonaventure and deserves reverence and respect.

5) They are grounded in compassionate love when they are grounded in Christ Crucified. For Bonaventure, to say that Christ is the center of our life is to say that all life emanates from the self-diffusive good of God. By emphasizing the good or love as the ground of all reality, Bonaventure introduced into the Franciscan tradition the theological roots of feminist theology.

IV. Franciscan Women Mystics: Neglected Voices of Theology

While Bonaventure's Christocentric world grounded in divine love undergirded a life-giving theology with a "feminist" world view, it did not last long in the tradition. Taken up in part by John Duns Scotus, it was ultimately eclipsed by an emphasis on Aristotelian ideas (such as perfect essential being, causality) and, eventually, Thomistic theology. However, it did survive "underground" in the voices and intense spiritual lives of Franciscan women. Mystics such as Clare of Assisi, Angela of Foligno, and Veronica Giuliani faithfully carried on an authentic Franciscan tradition of theology rooted in the good. By this I mean that their reflection of God as love led to the transformation of their lives and the world around them.

Margaret Carney tells us that a careful reading of women's *legendae* leads one to speculate on the congruence between themes found in the formal theological works of Franciscan friars and the spiritual experiences of women. At times, she says, the reader senses that what was formally proposed in a treatise or sermon by a learned friar theologian found its incarnate expression in the mystical experience or charitable endeavors of the women of Franciscan convents or monasteries.[25]

Certainly, we can see something of Carney's idea when we compare the writings of Clare and Bonaventure. Like Francis, Clare of Assisi desired to live a radical Gospel life following the footprints of Christ. Limited by ecclesiastical restrictions, Clare and her sisters pursued the Gospel life within the confines of the San Damiano convent. In her few letters to Agnes of Prague and in her Testament, Clare shows herself to be a courageous woman who desired to follow Christ wholeheartedly and to be joined to Christ as spouse. For Clare, relationship with Christ is the foundation of all authentic Christian relationships since it leads to relationships with others that are non-hierarchical and mutually affirming. She has a sense of *ekklesia* that is completely inclusive. Authority is not concentrated on control and power but in service to others. Love and service, following the example of Christ, signify Clare's way of living the evangelical life.

Clare's writings speak to us of incarnation, community, and the Gospel life, all of which are centered on the poor and humble Crucified Christ. For Clare, the love revealed in the Crucified is the source of joy, the ground of divine union, and the path to the fullness of life. Moreover, she viewed Christ Crucified as a mirror in which one could discover one's true image. By describing the Crucified as the true human image, she inadvertently broke with the classical Augustinian image of memory, intellect, and will and offered an authentic

---

[25]Carney, "Franciscan Women," 335.

Franciscan image of poverty, humility, and love. Clare's notion of the human image is original and theological. I believe it influenced Bonaventure, who elucidates this idea in his classic *Itinerarium Mentis in Deum*. As Marianne Schlosser says: "If Bonaventure read Clare's writings, he read them very well."[26] Clare and Bonaventure seem to have been kindred souls in accentuating the mystery of the cross.

Clare's theology, grounded in the experience of divine love, is found in other women mystics who followed her path. There is, for example, Angela of Foligno. Although she was an uneducated woman, her profound experience of God led her to the depths of the divine good. Like other women mystics, Angela discovered the path to love through the suffering humanity of Christ. In union with Christ, she discovered God as total love and all-embracing goodness, and came to realize that all created reality, including God's own Son, are gifts of God's self-diffusive goodness, giving life and drawing life back into the heart of the Trinity. This idea resonates with Bonaventure's metaphysics of emanation, exemplarity, and consummation (Hex. 1:17). The journey to God, as Angela describes it, is a journey into love. It begins with the gift of grace and culminates in the embrace of God's love. God's love embraces the soul so much that it produces bodily effects. The inner fire of love manifests itself bodily in the desire to suffer for another.

Angela's profound mystical experiences in union with Christ Crucified allowed her to understand that her true self and the truth of the whole created world exist only in being loved by the other, by God, who is a Trinity of love and who manifests this love in the sufferings of Jesus Christ. She describes the incarnation as the highest mystery brought about by the ineffable charity of the Trinity.[27] In her prayer for the seven gifts of the Creator, she prays for the gift of love. God is the gift above all other gifts, she says, because God *is* the gift and the gift is love made known to us in Jesus Christ.[28]

Angela's journey into the depths of divine love in Christ led her to articulate a profound theology of love. She discovered the very nature of God as love, the significance of this love as the ground of all created

---

[26]Marianne Schlosser, "Mother, Sister, Bride: The Spirituality of St. Clare," trans. Ignatius McCormick, *Greyfriars Review*, 5:2 (1991): 247.

[27]*Angela of Foligno: Complete Works*, trans. Paul Lachance (New York: Paulist, 1993), 308.

[28]*Angela of Foligno*, 311.

reality and the basis of her own human existence in the love of God. It is noteworthy that Angela attracted a circle of followers for whom she composed a body of *Instructions*. Even today she is remembered as a theologian. Her tomb in Foligno is engraved with the words: "The Theologian of Theologians."[29]

And then there is Veronica Giuliani, an eighteenth-century Poor Clare Capuchiness, who also perceived in the Crucified the full manifestation of divine love. Desiring to be united to God, Veronica conformed herself to Christ Crucified, eventually receiving the Stigmata. Her path of love, leading through suffering into the heart of God, led Veronica to mutually affirming relationships. Like Francis, she expressed her connection to the whole created world and invited the plants and stars to join her in praise of God.[30] Veronica discovered that love as the ground of existence enables one to experience freedom as right relationship with God and neighbor, obedience as loving charity to others, and authority as loving service to all. Like Clare, she experienced the good through union with Christ. As she grew in divine love, she was transformed in God. Love enabled her to see the goodness of every person and of the created world in the unity of Christ.

Clare, Angela, and Veronica allow us to assess the contribution of women mystics to Franciscan theology. Theirs is a true theology of praxis. It arises out of their personal experience and informs us about God, humanity, and the world. We can identify the characteristics of their theology as follows:

1) It is non-hierarchical. God is total love, not a Father who rules ruthlessly. In their writings, the mystics do not portray a God of domination and power; rather, they focus on God as love and overflowing goodness, which impels them to imitate this goodness in relation to others, especially in community.

2) It is non-dualistic. The women mystics viewed the human person as a dynamic unity and not as a dualistic dichotomy, that is, the body is not a part of the person but represents the person in one's totality. Identifying with the suffering humanity of Christ, women affirmed that God took on

---

[29]Carney, "Franciscan Women," 336.

[30]Lazaro Iriarte, "The Franciscan Spirit of St. Veronica Giuliani," trans. Edward Hagman, *Greyfriars Review*, 7:2 (1993): 226.

human flesh and, through the human body, opened up a path to divine love. Thus, they perceived the human body to be good and essential to the spiritual journey.

3) It has a sense of human dignity. Because women mystics had such a profound sense of the human person created by God, they showed respect for all persons as well as for the non-human created world. They did not experience a sense of inferiority or worthlessness but rather rejoiced in the fact that they, and all creation, were loved by God.

4) It incorporates kenosis or self-giving. The basis of all relationships for women mystics is compassionate love as expressed in Christ Crucified. The example of Christ revealed to them that the good is totally self-giving for the sake of the other. They did not view kenosis as submissiveness to dominating powers; rather, their self-giving became a means of empowerment and autonomy.

5) It is transformative. The lives of women mystics indicate that transformation of the self in the other, in Christ, leads to transformed relationships with one's neighbor and the non-human created world. Participation in the divine good through union with Christ leads one to a truly holistic view of the world and of one's self in the world.

6) It is comprehensive. Focusing on the good or love of God, women mystics perceived all material reality, including the human body, as an expression of the good; thus, they viewed all of creation as a sacrament of God.

In many ways, the writings of these women expressed a Franciscan worldview consonant with Bonaventure's theology, a theology centered on Christ, rooted in love, and oriented toward personhood and communion. The holistic and relational nature of their "practical theology," grounded in the love of God through union with Christ, can also be found in aspects of contemporary feminist theology.

V. Retrieving the Good: The Task of Women Today

If we accept the idea that Franciscan theology as a feminist liberating theology flourished underground in women mystics, we must also accept the fact that, after the Middle Ages, mainstream Franciscan theology became a mix of things—Bonaventure, Scotus, Aristotle, Aquinas, and a heavy dose of scholasticism all intersected to form "Franciscan theology." Some scholars claim Duns Scotus is the theologian *par excellence* of the Franciscan Order. George Marcil, for example, says that Scotus became to Franciscans what Thomas was to Dominicans.[31] Even if this is the case, the tradition of the good as the ground of a Franciscan theological world view was lost to the mainstream. Franciscan theology not only acquired Aquinas's God of perfect being, but it also lost its significance as a theology of praxis, that is, as the ground of personal transformation. Knowledge became divorced from love. This direction was supported by Pope Leo XIII's encyclical *Aeterni Patris* (1879), which mandated Thomistic theology as the official theology of all seminaries, Catholic colleges and universities.[32] Rather than knowledge for the sake of deepening love, Franciscan theology became a purely intellectual endeavor. It was written in a language that only few could write, and it espoused ideas that only few could understand. Moreover, theologians came to live comfortably in two worlds—the world-at-large of Thomas Aquinas and the textbook world of Bonaventure and Scotus. This type of schizophrenia left Franciscans in abeyance and, in a sense, betrayed the original Franciscan charism. Friars trained for clerical ministry knew Thomas's *Summa* in its entirety, but the works of Bonaventure and Scotus only in brief. Women were virtually excluded from any knowledge of these works.

If we accept the idea that a schizophrenic identity evolved with the dissolution of the original charism itself, we might also suggest that the early Franciscan movement, characterized by a sense of mutual relationships between men and women, maintained a theology of praxis that can be read today as feminist and liberating. As the relationships between men and women suffered from a consolidation of hierarchy and power, so too did Franciscan theology fall between the cracks of various intellectual thinkers.

Part of the restoration of authentic Franciscan theology in our time, and perhaps the most significant part, is the inclusion of women in

---

[31]George Marcil, OFM, "The Franciscan School through the Centuries," in *History of Franciscan Theology*, 317. Marcil's article favors Scotus as the "connecting link" in the history of Franciscan theology.

[32]Marcil, 325.

Franciscan studies. This is significant not only as a means of rectifying the mutuality of relationships in the tradition but because the very nature of Franciscan theology as relational and holistic means that its health depends on the mutual relationships of men and women. Moreover, the lives of women mystics indicate to us that women have an affinity for the tradition of the good which underscores a relational theology.

It is not surprising that a number of women today are attracted to Bonaventure's theology. Speaking for myself, I can say that I gravitated toward Bonaventure not because he was a towering intellectual or philosopher but because his theological world view with Christ as center is held together by compassionate love. My attraction for Bonaventure's theology was initially my attraction for the good or divine love as the ground of reality. In this respect, I feel akin to Angela and Veronica—not because I am a visionary mystic but because like them I see the good as the essential meaning of all reality. Although I have not spoken at length with lay women to assess their attraction to Franciscan theology, I would venture to say that their interest in the tradition is probably associated with the good that underscores the liberating feminist principles within this theology.

It is interesting to speculate that in the last fifty years or so Franciscan theology has undergone an *aggiornamento* or, better yet, a renaissance. With the resurgence of critical studies on Franciscan texts and the admission of women to graduate degree programs, Franciscan theology is being born anew. The Franciscan Institute, begun in 1940, was the first in this country to open its doors to women in Franciscan studies. Even before the official opening of the Institute, women at St. Bonaventure University, such as Emma Thérèse Healy, pursued doctoral degrees in Franciscan theology. Healy's well-known translation of Bonaventure's *De reductione theologiam ad artium* is still referred to today.

With the changes in religious life after Vatican II, the number of women who obtained degrees in Franciscan studies became significant. A list of graduates of the Franciscan Institute between the years 1975 and 1990 shows a high number of women obtaining master's degrees in Franciscan studies. In the class of 1978, for example, all but one of the graduates were women; in the class of 1983, all four of the graduates were women.[33] Many of these women returned to their communities to help educate them in the Franciscan charism. Several went on to pursue doctoral degrees. Franciscan publications such as *The Cord* furthered the involvement of women in Franciscan studies. Joseph Doino, long-time editor of *The Cord*, said that both Franciscan men and women contributed to it from its beginning in an effort to update Franciscan spirituality.[34]

Today, programs in Franciscan studies such as those at the Washington Theological Union, the Franciscan Institute, and the Franciscan School of Theology at Berkeley are aiding the rebirth of the tradition. I can personally say that our Franciscan brother scholars have been welcoming and encouraging with regard to women in Franciscan studies. Their efforts to be inclusive of women and to look toward women for original contributions to the field reflect a sense of what the original Franciscan charism is about. In a broader context, scholars who are not members of a religious order but contributors to Franciscan studies have also made a difference with regard to the inclusion of women. Here I am thinking of Ewert Cousins of Fordham University, whose lifelong interest in things Franciscan has inspired a number of women to pursue doctoral dissertations in Franciscan theology.

Much of what I am saying here is not exclusive to women but intended for all men and women who are interested in the tradition. At the same time, I feel the moment of women in Franciscan theology has arrived. As our world shifts away from a mechanistic world, a Thomistic world, a world that emphasizes being and individualism and moves toward a holistic world, a relational world, a Bonaventurian world, a world of the good, the contribution of women to the articulation of a meaningful Franciscan theology is vital. We are beginning to see a new era where women are not only contributing to theology but are reshaping the way we think about theology.

Our efforts at this conference to articulate Franciscan theology as a feminist liberating theology is a case in point. On a broader level, women are studying the tradition not only with a view toward retrieving the voices of women who have been suppressed, but with a view toward equality, mutuality, and integration. Here I would point out the work of

---

[33]See *Franciscan Studies: The Franciscan Institute Fiftieth Anniversary Edition*, 51 (1991): 209, 211.

[34]Joseph Doino, OFM, "The Cord," *Franciscan Studies* 51 (1991): 134.

Margaret Carney, Roberta McKelvie, Ingrid Peterson, and Elizabeth Petroff among others. To ensure the success of these endeavors, Franciscan studies must continuously be developed with a hermeneutic of suspicion, questioning all areas that betray the good and thus the authenticity of the tradition itself. A critical interpretation of Franciscan theology must seek to restore the good by restoring theology as praxis, that is, as a theology that shapes our daily lives. In this respect theologians must maintain a dialectic between interpreting the experiences of Francis and Clare and serious, critical theological reflection on a troubled world. As Zachary Hayes says:

> There is a sense in which we may see the relation between Francis and the theologians of the order such as Bonaventure as a relationship between intense, personal, religious experience on the one hand, and serious, sustained, critical reflection on the other. When we look at the roots of the Franciscan tradition from this perspective, we are challenged not simply to retrieve the experience of Francis: we are challenged as well to retrieve the spirit of critical, constructive reflection on that experience.[35]

In view of this relationship between reflecting on Francis's experience and doing critical theological reflection, I see four areas where women are making important differences in the renewal of Franciscan theology:

1) Teaching. Women now have an opportunity to influence Franciscan theology from within the walls of the academy both from the point of critical reflection and of pedagogy. Teaching is an important area for women, who can now contribute both to the content of Franciscan theology and the manner in which theology is taught. In this respect, the theologian is to be not only a source of knowledge but also a role model of the type of theology espoused—the theologian must somehow embody the good and express

---

[35]Hayes, "Franciscan Wisdom Tradition," 37; cf. Pompei ("*Sermones* of St. Anthony," 302) who states that "a Franciscan theologian is anyone who, beginning from a well-defined religious perspective and faithful to Francis's spirit of freedom, humility and love, shows a readiness and ability to enter into the great contemporary questions. Using the language and categories of the time, he or she is able to bring these questions face to face with the demands of the gospel."

this in didactic relationships. I believe that the development of a Franciscan method of teaching based on the good can enable theology as praxis to be more fully realized.

2) Writing. Since the admission of women to Franciscan studies, women have made significant contributions through writing. While there are various levels of research and writing, I believe the most influential are those which are critically evaluating the tradition and seeking to restore its authenticity in all areas.

3) Public Speaking. Opportunities to give presentations and to speak publicly are being afforded women, and these offer valuable arenas for discussion of Franciscan theology in the public sphere. It is one way of bringing theology "out of the ranks and into the files." Moreover, it is a way of bringing Franciscans of the various orders as well as all other persons interested in the tradition into meaningful dialogue. In order to facilitate a theology of praxis that can influence and transform Christian life, Franciscan studies must continuously move in this direction. Considering the efforts of the Franciscan Federation, I think women are already making a difference in this regard.

4) Joint Ventures. A number of women today are participating in joint colloquiums or seminars of men and women who are bringing the Franciscan tradition into dialogue with the contemporary world. These discussions signify the desire to restore the sphere of mutual relationships within the tradition and reveal a type of exchange that is enriching for the tradition and for the church.

As we continue to move forward in this rebirth, Franciscan theology must remain centered on Jesus Christ as the fulcrum of theological discourse. The key to Franciscan theology as a liberating theology is bound up in the mystery of Christ. I find the words of Catherine LaCugna particularly apt in this regard:

Jesus Christ remains the sole criterion of human personhood, and God's Holy Spirit remains the sole means by which authentic person hood is achieved. . . . The Christian feminist concern for nonhierarchical relationships based on the mutuality and reciprocity of persons equal in dignity must, from a theological standpoint, remain rooted in the stories of salvation through Jesus Christ. [36]

Only by discovering a Christ who is the wisdom of God can the tradition of the good be fully restored as a meaningful tradition for our time. The restoration of the good in Franciscan theology offers hope based on compassionate love to a world of individualism, violence, and ecological destruction. Theology is to enable one to embody the good in one's attitudes and actions, not in words alone, and to be a compassionate co-pilgrim accompanying people in their journey to full life. Such hope is thwarted, however, if, as theologians, we hide away in books and barricade ourselves in intellectual knowledge or, as followers of Francis, we look for the ladder to climb to heaven. That ladder has come down, Bonaventure states, in the person of Jesus Christ: Christ, love, and liberation cannot be separated. Both Francis and Clare realized this. Francis praised God as the supreme good and kissed the leper while Clare gazed on Christ and washed the feet of her sisters. Bonaventure pondered the mystery of Christ as the God of love while Scotus saw love as the reason for Christ. For Franciscans, love is the meaning of God and God's love, revealed in Christ, is the meaning of the world.

As Franciscan theology enters into a new millennium, the new birth that has begun must give rise to new life in the Church. Both women and men in Franciscan theology today must have the same goal as feminist theologians. They must seek to incorporate Franciscan theology into the Church not simply as another theology but as the operative theology of Christian life. To do this, theologians and Franciscans alike must be sensitive to all that strips the world of the created good and bring this to task. I believe that some are already pursuing this challenge. If we nurture this new birth, then what we are doing today will be the cause of joy for the Church of tomorrow.

---

[36]LaCugna, "God in Communion with Us," 92.

Speaking a Woman's Vision:
Feminist and/or Franciscan?
Response to Ilia Delio

Gabriele Uhlein, OSF

"I am not a feminist, I am a Franciscan." A woman theologian recently said these words while we were considering together the various components of an upcoming seminar that was entitled *Franciscan Studies: the Difference Women Are Making.* Striking was my own intuitive response: "I am a Franciscan feminist." Between these two positions is a vast territory for fertile conversation (and perhaps the positions are not as divergent as a first hearing might suggest). Yet that there is a press to define ourselves differently, both of us as contemporary theologians and Franciscans, points up the need for further analysis. As Bonnie Miller-McLemore (1998) has observed, the landscape of theological reflection, textual analysis, and pastoral praxis will never be the same again. Women's voices in the study of religion and spirituality at all levels have

> exposed the misogyny embedded in traditions and institutions which have characterized women as emotionally juvenile, morally and intellectually inferior, and spiritually evil. [They have] interrogated the very categories and customs that define religion. . . (p. 1).

I count myself fortunate to have never been without these voices and to have had the fertile possibility of fashioning a feminist voice of my own. To use the term "feminist" now requires careful explanation and attention, lest the voices of the many different and hard-won perspectives of women be arrogantly blurred once again. But to analyze the various perspectives of the feminist voices present in the theological and religious geography is not mine to do here. Rather, I will simply identify my own position and eagerly anticipate a further mutual shaping of the spiritual landscape we all share. There is a poem by Emily Dickenson that has recently been haunting me. It succinctly captures the power and the urgency of bringing the various feminist positions to the table of discourse within the Franciscan family:

> A word is dead
> When it is said,
> Some say.
> I say it just
> Begins to live
> That day.

Here Emily Dickenson vividly expresses the intuition that words do indeed *live* when they are *said*. Hence my joy and eagerness to participate with others in a conversation regarding the differences women, *as women*, are actually making in Franciscan studies. I was given pause, however, by the next descriptive line on the printed announcement that described the proposed event as: "a distinguished group of scholars." The names listed on the program, including my own, all conclude with a Franciscan suffix. That they do so is to be celebrated, but that they are listed as "distinguished" and as "scholars" merits careful consideration. Not that they ought not be recognized as such; their achievements are to be recognized. Rather, my aim here is to call attention to a fundamental tension between cherished Franciscan values (e.g. humility and minority, etc.) and our own resonant participation in serious intellectual discourse within the broader realm of Religion as academic discipline. The question each of us who are listed here must answer for ourselves is how we can, with personal integrity as Franciscans, be identified as "distinguished scholars" in a tradition of "humility and minority."

Over the past twenty years of vowed membership within the Franciscan family, I have developed a "litmus test" of sorts for discerning "what is mine to do." I ask myself if I can imagine Francis or Clare, or my foundress, approving the action. I ask if Bonaventure or Scotus might support my logic. I consider the impact it will have on community life and earth resources, and I seek the counsel of my sisters and other women. That I do this reflects my post-Vatican II religious formation. I have always had access to English language Franciscan sources. The only rule I know is the current *Form of Life of the Sisters and Brothers of the Third Order Regular*. I have been given opportunity to cultivate an eco-feminist consciousness that is supported by both my Franciscan tradition and the contemporary social teachings of the Church. I have never been without the encouragement and example of other Franciscan women scholars. And, by virtue of my academic education, I now have a "doctoral" voice in theological conversation. All these facts are significant to the tensions I feel as a Franciscan eco-feminist and as a participating so-named "distinguished scholar" in this conversation regarding the difference women are making in Franciscan studies.

The second area of tension in this conversation is the fact that Francis, Clare, Bonaventure, and Scotus were not feminists, Franciscan or otherwise. Yet I do claim such an identity. The tensions of this position I embrace gladly. Significantly, to do so is possible *only in this era*. I am indebted in this effort not only to the feminist critique in general, but also to specific Franciscans such as Margaret Carney, Ilia Delio, Roberta McKelvie, and Ingrid Peterson, who generously and willingly share their insights as Franciscan women scholars. I must also add that I do not come to this dialogue from within the discipline of Franciscan studies. I am a depth psychologist and a process theologian whose work is further informed by eco-feminist voices (voices that specifically link feminist concerns with ecological issues). That I am given opportunity to participate in this conversation bespeaks the willing inclusive wisdom that Franciscan women have already brought to our internal familial dialogue.

We sisters and brothers, shaping and incarnating Franciscan thought today, can never again be without women's voices. And the words of Franciscan women continue to live because they continue to be said. And given that our words do "live," it is my intent here to revisit the individual "living" components of the phrase "Franciscan Studies: the Difference Women Are Making" in the context of my own experience as a participant in this forum.

"Franciscan Studies": the "Within" Question

As someone who identifies herself as a Franciscan woman, I must ask the question: "What difference does it make?" My presumption is that women in Franciscan Studies can, and indeed ought, contribute to that feminist agenda that has at its most basic core the struggle to end sexist oppression. As feminist author bell hooks (1984) has expressed it, the feminist aim

> is not to benefit solely any specific group of women, any particular race or class of women. It does not privilege women over men. It has the power to transform in a meaningful way all of our lives (p. 26).

For me the power that Franciscan studies holds is precisely its transforming power. I have been profoundly changed by it. And it is precisely because of my Franciscan study that I name myself an eco-feminist. The very best of the Franciscan tradition has taught me to honor and incarnate the *Word*, with careful attention and much affection. Franciscan studies has taught me to tend and to love the "texts"—the Gospel, our Franciscan "sources," and the "non-verbals" of our creaturely kin. And all this presumes a particular "living" literacy that flies in the face of the persistently reductionistic traditional analysis of most academic enterprises.

Yet in contemporary feminist religious studies there is a cause for concern that has recently surfaced in the field of biblical hermeneutics in particular. According to J. D. H. Amador in the Spring 1998 issue of the *Journal of the American Academy of Religion*, there can be in feminist biblical hermeneutics a peculiar "failure of theoretical nerve"—that is, the trap of over-analysis, a "limiting the focus to textuality and 'meaning'" (p. 41). To limit the discussion in this way to an interpretation of the intended "meaning" of the text alone, without also engaging in a discussion of the intended effect of the textual interpretation, is insufficient. The caveat is well taken. In Franciscan studies too, the temptation to focus only on textual meanings and the comparative values of theories of interpretation is ever present. As Amador writes, the unfortunate result is a spate of articles and books in which

> . . . interpreters are caught in a trap of having to argue over the academic interests of "methods" and "meanings" and "theories," to write more and more texts, to generate more and more commentaries and critiques. Meanwhile, the sisters for whom we are engaging in the necessary task of critical analytical practice are waiting for us to join them in the very real struggles and battles that are being waged

against all of us, waiting for us to provide them with the important insights and strategies of power at work in biblical androcentric ideology and practices. . . (p. 53).

Hence, from a properly feminist perspective, it is not enough to ask what did Francis and Clare "mean," or even what did Jesus "mean" in their own particular context, without taking into account the very real pragmatic experiences that color our approach to the text, shape what we will be saying about the text, and determine what we want our intended audience to assume to be true. These are important considerations, since to ascribe "meaning" is ultimately *authoritative in intention*. Text, especially religious text, is "alive." Its authors and its interpreters each intend authority. There is no such thing as disinterested religious scholarship, or for that matter, disinterested Franciscan studies. Each attempt made at discerning the "meaning" of a particular text seeks to claim its own share of powerful authority in the present community for which the scholarship is undertaken. The gift of the feminist critique is to question the motives of that authority.

It jolts my more "romantic" sensibilities to think that Francis and Clare had ideological, rhetorical intent in their appropriation of sacred scripture—as do I, and as do we, even when we gather for something so "non-academic" as a communal scripture sharing. The important "out-come" is not so much what we share, but *that* we share, and that our sharing together impacts and affects our lives. Here we too appropriate scripture to make a difference "in the world," and here too we are in good company. What Jesus, what Francis and Clare desired was not "words" but action. Franciscan studies, then, like scripture studies, are not primarily for "truth and method"—they are for "truth and power." They are for the incarnation of the *Word* in transformative action, that is, to move the intended audience to act. For me, this insight is the "pearl of great price" in Franciscan studies and a treasure we can contribute to the rising feminist consciousness.

Franciscan studies requires of its scholars a gospel-formed "fioretti" sensitivity and skill. It presumes the capacity both to attend to and to tell a story as a change agent. It requires of the teller personal affectivity, specificity, and awareness of transformational intent. No exegesis is "presumption-less." To use the power of Franciscan storytelling with integrity requires that as a feminist, I ask what those presumptions are—particularly as the traditional stories are told, the memories are cherished, and new episodes are folded into the Franciscan family history we share and continue to create together. Franciscan studies then, ought to be transformative rhetoric in the best possible sense of the term—a story, a text, a *Word* as an incarnately conscious, intentional communication. Moreover, this sort of communication requires me to be pragmatic, persuasive, and transformationally engaged with the listening participants in the complexity and the risk of mutual dialog.

It is clear that Franciscan studies ought not be for the development of an exegetically skillful and adroit Franciscan theology alone. It ought also evoke the lived experience of the transforming *"Word made flesh"* among us—and most particularly, ought to affirm that *Word* where it is most presumed to be absent. I would call it gospel "Incarnation" in a circle widest cast. Feminist Franciscan scholars thus ought ask not only what the specific texts of Jesus or Francis or Clare or Angela, etc. "mean." They ought also commit to a conscious examination of what lures them to study these texts in the first place.

For example, as I consider the Franciscan sources, I must reflect on the motives I bring to the academic enterprise, as well as what the texts evoke in my affective life, in my relationships, and in the various groups to which I belong and to which I relate. Because of the sexist and classist traditions in which our Franciscan sources are embedded, there will be both dissonances and congruencies with my experience. While the congruencies will afford us consolation as Franciscans, the sensitive and thoughtful exploration of the dissonances will afford us our best Franciscan hope. Only then will we participate with integrity in the transformational power of the *Word*. Harking back to my initial opening reflection, I might claim the title "distinguished scholar" as a feminist Franciscan, only if "distinguished" implies "transformationally significant" and "scholar" implies attentive "student"—a title certainly available to anyone willing to risk the rigors of learning and of transformative conversion.

Regarding "women in"

There are in our Franciscan family fascinating recollections and stories, even from the very beginning, of what to do with "the women." Certainly, to find a more central and mutual place today for women's voices within Franciscan studies will be a project fraught with cultural contradictions and presumed orthodox universals. This is not a situation that is unique to the Franciscan academic project. Although the boundaries may be in flux, women's voices within theological discourse in general have not been from the central presiding position. Rather, they come from the edges of the table, if not from exile itself (be it forced or voluntary). To complicate matters, there is no one general feminist "voice," and appropriately so. Women have long been aware of the negation of precious individual "difference" in the patriarchally presumed simplicity of reducing the "many" individuated voices to "one" adversarial minority position.

However, while the chorus of many women's voices may seem disconcertingly pluralistic, these voices from the edges or from exile are in concert in their capacity to expose the fallible "universalism" of presumed generalities that "ghettoize" non-androcentric perspectives. As Katie Geneva Cannon (1995) has emphasized, there is a "moral agency" to the exiled voice. In *Katie's Canon*, she speaks to the absurdity of the institutionalized "inferiority of the marginalized" by using the lived experience of "the least of them"—in her case poor, Black, working women—to expose the structures that presume to legitimate their exclusion. Cannon describes a marginalization that takes its toll in the particulars of individual black female flesh and blood. To those of us formed by a Franciscan telling of the Gospel texts, surely we are to attend, consciously and *in particular*, to the marginalized voice "of the least of these," no matter which "ism" (racist, sexist, homophobic, etc.) constitutes the exclusion. Here, on the edges and amid the exiles, Franciscans can find their own feminist congruence and transformative pedagogy of transformation.

As a Franciscan, I must deal with injustice and the hypocrisy of concretized generalizations. There is no one voice to speak for the whole, and if we do not welcome the "lepers" to the table we shall never know the Christ/Word that is theirs to speak. Perhaps it is too easy to "see" the marginalization of the "lepers" and to picture romantically the other-worldly happy brothers and sisters of Francis tending to their needs. What is required is an awareness that recognizes this ministry to the leper "exiles" *as a praxis and pedagogy* profoundly disturbing to the good people of Assisi. Including women's voices at the Franciscan study-table ought to be equally provocative *as a praxis and pedagogy* for the pursuit of such studies. Moreover, if we are true to our own non-linear fioretti pedagogy of honoring personal experience, Franciscan students at this table ought to be less likely to label or dismiss or misunderstand the work of women. Are not these women's voices "minor" voices? As long as women (and any other category of "exiles") can only speak in "minor" voices, I am, as a Franciscan, compelled to attend. This is the unsettling and transformational reality of Francis and of any Franciscan studies as I understand them.

To be fair, I must acknowledge that such "unsettling" is indeed underway regarding women's voices in general. Even a cursory comparison of the editorial boards of some leading journals in religious studies reveals this. *The Journal of the American Academy of Religion* and our own Franciscan *Greyfriars Review* each have an editorial staff that is one third female, while *The Journal of Pastoral Theology* and the Franciscan journal, *The Cord*, have editorial staffs that are 50% and 60% women respectively. The first two journals are considered more "theoretical." It is worth noting that though they have a lower percentage of women's participation in the editorial process than *The Journal of Pastoral Theology* and the *The Cord*, the statistics are nonetheless indicative of a hopeful transformational shift in gender-specific voice.

The "difference" . . .

From a Franciscan feminist perspective, the "minor" voice as a change agent cannot be over emphasized. Should women's voices be fully incorporated eventually, there will always be other "minor" voices at the margin. Hence the power of a Franciscan pedagogy that consciously listens to the exiled and therefore potentially "subversive" voice. For example, as an eco-feminist, I can imagine

The Canticle of the Creatures being sung today in just such a minor tone. To understand my universe place as one of cosmic kith and kin and then to embody that truth in a presentationally immediate way as Francis and Clare did is surely a subversive harmony in a world economy driven by multi-national corporate interests. Moreover, to extol peace in the midst of conflict and ultimately to embrace even dying with equanimity certainly subverts prevailing cultural standards and beliefs. What is significant is not that Francis sang *The Canticle*, but that he gave incarnate reality to it. Francis lived *The Canticle*, used it as a pedagogical device, and fully expected those after him to do likewise. Francis used his song to teach his followers how to live transformatively in the midst of alienation, of conflict, and of death. Therein lies *The Canticle*'s power.

Also as a feminist Franciscan, I am compelled to acknowledge the diversities of agenda among feminists themselves. Interestingly enough, these distinctions parallel divisions that can be found within the Franciscan family as well. The necessary but not exhaustive list of descriptions ranges from those who would describe themselves as conciliatory or as humanist to those self-identified as more politicized and/or more radical in their agenda. If anything, such distinctions remind me again that no one woman can speak for all women. As a result, it is equally clear that no one Franciscan can speak for all Franciscans. For example, just as there are cultural and humanist positions regarding poverty, so there are those positions that are more political or more radical in their agenda and choice of communal expression.

Perhaps it is here in community, amid much diversity of position and attitude, that we can find ourselves face to face with no less than the connective genius hidden in the seemingly insurmountable Franciscan struggle to live a common life. In community, regardless of its constitution, I am challenged to find the "other," the one not myself, the different voice. This clearly moves my feminist Franciscan studies praxis, much as it moves my understanding of poverty (or of contemplation or of any of the Franciscan virtues, for that matter) from the realm of the academic and theoretical into the "perfect joy" of the specific, the pragmatic, and the incarnate actual, where Franciscans have always been most at home. Moreover, Franciscan studies, if true to its "minor" voice, has the obligation to challenge (and some would say "disrupt") the presumed boundaries that comprise any prevailing notions of exclusivity and privilege.

Of course, there are concomitant caveats. The trap of "minor" elitism is ever present. There is, too, the problematic question: "Should the Franciscan perspective become 'mainstream' would it still be Franciscan?" While there is no evidence for this happening in the near future, the point is well taken. It points to the fundamentally transformative aspect of both feminist and Franciscan pedagogy and its fundamentally "subversive" character. Sandra Harding (1986), in her essay "The Instability of the Analytical Categories of Feminist Theory," suggests that we must develop the skills necessary to hold variety, distinction, contradiction, and the insecurities of nonstability as positive values. At the same time, it behooves us to eschew pat answers and firmly fixed categories that both hinder our capacity to understand each other and determine our socially approved behaviors. Certainly there are here in Harding's recipe, descriptors familiar to Franciscans. From our own fioretti we can hear a resonance—the actions of Francis and Clare were nothing if not counter distinctive and contradictory to the prevailing logic of thirteenth-century Assisi. Franciscan pedagogy through the centuries has done no less than allow us to continue to hold the paradoxical and temporal non-securities of our founders as virtuous. If anything, Franciscans know how to tell the story of variety, distinction, contradiction and the insecurities of nonstability very well.

"Making" something of it all . . .

There is no mystery sweeter in Franciscan theological reflection than that of the Incarnation. Hence Franciscan studies, not only from a pragmatic feminist perspective but also from a profound mystical imperative, must be Incarnationally accountable. If we are to "make something" of the world, if we are to preach, to critique, to offer an alternative "voice," it ought be done responsibly and from a suitably humble position. Moreover, if the choice is to engage theologically, there is no excuse for theological naivete. This requires us to understand that whether the theoretical orientation be that of a "believer" or a "skeptic," an "insider" or an "outsider," there is no privileged place of "neutral" observation. My own study will always take form in the peculiar specifics of my own flesh and blood reality. Thus our contemporary form of Franciscan studies will need to practice certain incarnation skills, even as the Religious Studies Academy as a whole must learn to incorporate them. Fiona Bowie (1998) suggests that foremost among these skills is a willingness "to disrupt patriarchal boundaries" in an ethically accountable manner; that is, to acknowledge and encourage plural voices, to cherish

> their participation based on respect for others and mediated by certain ethical demands. (Overtly racist, sexist, ageist or homophobic politics for example have no place. . . .) These ethical standpoints may be contingent and open to negotiation, but the building of community and the joyful expression of the individual's energies will be at the basis of [such] an ethical approach (p. 61).

In addition, as Elizabeth Schüssler Fiorenza and Emilie Townes (1998) recently indicated, "seeing is always partial; feminists have never taken to the idea of a God's-eye view" (p. 1). Domains and disciplines interweave, much as praxis and pedagogy must in an incarnate Franciscan studies enterprise. They go on to suggest that the religious studies scholar, Franciscan or otherwise, must not only promote the full humanity of those created in God's image and likeness. The scholar is also required "to come to terms with her own beliefs, her agenda, her social location, and its attendant interests, as well as the power dynamics" (p. 2) of her teaching role and style of exchange. Taking responsibility for my own scholarship then, requires me to be as transparent as I can be regarding my own Franciscan scholarly agenda.

I must clearly identify my contributions as that of an eco-feminist and recognize as well that my own particular Franciscan formation gives my eco-feminist voice a unique tenor. In addition, I must admit my partiality to process theology, the cosmological vision of Thomas Berry and Brian Swimme, and the spiritual sensibilities of the Rhineland mystics. Thus the metaphors of growth and complexity, of evolution and ongoing creativity frame for me a suitable language for a cosmic Christology that speaks to *my* heart and captures *my* enthusiasm. For example, I might more comfortably speak of Bonaventure's "self-diffusive good" as the divine lure to increasing complexity and relatedness. Likewise, given the centrality of the Christ in the Franciscan theological corpus, I might affirm a Christology that appreciates "difference" as a graced opportunity for increased possibilities of relatedness and novel connections. In this I am supported by a sure Franciscan faith that all is ultimately held together in Christ.

My scholastic agenda therefore, will include dialogue with the natural sciences, attention to ecological imperatives, and a trust of organic spontaneities over linear logic. And I expect to be changed by my engagement with the texts, the students, and other co-participants in the Franciscan studies enterprise. Hence my criteria for ministry—a fully participative process of conscious creativity and ecological embodiment in the lineage of Francis and Clare. Herein are revealed my biases and my preferences, my particular enfleshing of the ever living *Word*. This is what I contribute differently. This is what informs my desire to join in conversation with other scholars.

Consequently, I can conclude that full and mutually transformative participation is ultimately the praxis that best expresses such an incarnation pedagogy. In this regard, I particularly value the contribution of those involved in Franciscan studies. They are the ones that will afford us references for our ongoing stories and offer us roots and connections should we wish them. These women and men, as the conservators and interpreters of our past, provide no less than the means with which to meet consciously the uncharted future as Franciscans. This will require of those pursuing Franciscan studies, positions resonant with various feminist agenda:

- Franciscan scholars, especially those pursuing Franciscan studies are challenged to write and teach for flesh and blood persons in embodied circumstances and not for an abstract disembodied public. In doing so they may well risk their own exile from the Religious Studies Academy at large, and other more traditional Franciscans in particular, as they attend to, and identify with, the "minor" voice.

- Franciscan studies is most powerful when "the text" being studied is engaged not as a "product," but rather as a catalyst for "Christ-centered" change, both of the scholar and of those seeking to learn from the scholar's work. Engaging the text presumes thereby an openness to transformation. It does not necessarily presume the defense of a predetermined position. Moreover, the mutual participation of both student and teacher is implied. It is not the text, per se, that is the occasion of this transformative grace, but rather the mutual living engagement of it.

- While it is foreseeable that some various feminist agenda presently at the edges of the religious studies conversation will indeed eventually become mainstream, the Franciscan agenda, if true to its call to "minority," consistently ought to seek out the voices of "the least among us." The Franciscan studies agenda ought never "arrive" or finish or become "mainstream." The voices of our "exiles" ought never cease to challenge or disrupt presumed boundaries, never cease to introduce new relationships, and ever deepen our community connections.

- Such radical community will require rigorous study and conscious, careful cultivation of non-essentialist intentional relationships. The willingness to struggle to remain connected and the resultant richness of communal diversity ought be our hallmark.

The feminist position in the Religious Studies Academy itself is already marked both by such struggle and by such wealth. There are the *mujeristas*, the *womanists*, the Euro-American feminists, the Asian feminists, the gay/lesbian feminists, and the differently-abled feminists. There may well be as many distinctive voices as there are individual womanly incarnations. What affords me hope in this plethora of perspectives is the fact that within the Franciscan family, and particularly for me in the Third Order Regular, all these voices are indeed already recognizably present. We continue, for the most part successfully, to remain in community. We continue to be wonderfully true to our communal commitments. And we continue to look to our tradition to sustain us, not to conserve the past rigidly, but to study it, to engage it, and to enflesh it in newly transformative ways.

Our very capacity for community building will depend upon our tradition—not in the abstract, but in the incarnate concrete. It will require no less than a creative pedagogy that holds in sensitive concert, as only exiles can, the diverse and messy particulars of our lives. A good *Word* that "lives" as it is said—that is the best hope of Franciscan scholarship, particularly now that Franciscan women are finding their own rich and varied voices. Franciscans ought never be the same again. And as this *Word* is said, it will begin that day to live—more beautifully than any single Franciscan of either gender could ever have imagined.

References

Amador, J. D. H. "Feminist Biblical Hermeneutics: a Failure of Theoretical Nerve." *Journal of the American Academy of Religion*, 66.1. Spring, 1998. 39-53.

Bowie, Fiona. "Trespassing on Sacred Domains: A Feminist Anthropological Approach to Theology and the Study of Religions." *Feminist Studies in Religion*, 14.1. Spring, 1998. 40-62.

Cannon, Katie Geneva. *Katie's Canon: Womanism and the Soul of the Black Community*. New York: Continuum, 1995.

Dickenson, Emily. *Poems, Second Series*. Ed. Mabel Lewis Todd and Thomas Wentworth Higginson. New York: Crown Publishers, 1978.

Fiorenza, Elizabeth Schüssler and Emilie Townes. "Editors Introduction." *Feminist Studies in Religion*. Spring, 1998, 14.1. 40-62.

Harding, Sandra "The Instability of the Analytical Categories of Feminist Theory." *Signs*, 11.4. 1986. 645-642.

hooks, bell. *Feminist Theory: From Margin to Center*. Boston: South End, 1984.

Miller-McLemore, Bonnie. "Feminist Theory in Pastoral Theology." *Association of Practical Theology Occasional Papers*. Fall, 1998.

Studies of Medieval Franciscan Women: Current French and Italian Scholarship

Paul Lachance, OFM

In *Zen and the Art of Motor Cycle Maintenance*, a counter-culture best-seller which appeared in 1974, the protagonist, a philosopher-motorcycle biker, is reflecting on the journey across America he has taken with his son. He makes the following observation on what they have seen:

> There's this primary America of freeways and jet flights and TV and movie spectaculars. And people caught up in this primary America seem to go through huge portions of their lives without much consciousness of what's immediately around them. The media has convinced them that what is around them is unimportant. And that's why they are lonely. . . . But in the secondary America we've been through, of back roads, and Chinaman's ditches, and Appaloosa horses, and sweeping mountain ranges, and meditative thoughts, and kids with pinecones and bumblebees and open sky above us mile after mile, all through that, what was real, what was *around* us dominated. And so there wasn't much feeling of loneliness.[1]

Franciscans, by vocation, are meant to be part of secondary America, the roads not taken, where those "by the wayside" live. In my own case, it is certainly while erring in the back alleys of my own life that the salutation came to work on Angela of Foligno, or more appropriately to let Angela weave her spell over me: "You will be entrusted with sons and daughters," she was told, "on this side of the sea and beyond it." Initially, I thought I would pursue my research in

---

[1]Robert M. Pirsig, *Zen and the Art of Motorcycle Maintenance* (New York: Morrow, 1974).

The present text of this article is rooted in an oral presentation. Subsequently references were added, but certain titles—particularly those of periodicals and encyclopedic works—have not been documented in full. The editor added sufficient information for the concerned reader to retrieve important sources of this presentation. The author is willing to supply further information upon request: e-mail address: Plachance@worldnet.att.net.; mailing address: 1117 N. Hoyne St. Chicago, Il. 60622. Most of the translations from Italian and French texts in this paper are the author's.

57

Berkeley, but, in the early seventies, interest in mystics was still at a low ebb, particularly those whom few in the English-speaking world had ever heard about. I found no one in Berkeley to support my project. So, reluctantly, and with considerable trepidation, I abandoned the soft "cushy bed" which was mine as chaplain of the Christian Brothers (their novitiate) winery in the Napa valley, to move to the considerably more harshly-meshed cots of the Pontificium Athenaeum Antonianum in Rome. Perseverance on "the path of thorns and tribulations" led to the publication of my thesis, followed by the Classics volume, and more recently, in collaboration with Thaddée Matura and Jean-François Godet, the French version of Angela's writings.[2]

While in Italy, *mirabile dictu*, not on the *viali principali*, to be sure, but on the *stradetti e vicoli*, I not only became enamored of *gli italiani* and *cose italiane*, but also became increasingly impressed by the quality of Italian scholarship, in particular the research on Franciscans and Franciscanism. The spectacular growth of contemporary Italian historical scholarship certainly parallels its English counterpart, and in the Franciscan area, in fact, it considerably surpasses it. In this essay, I cannot hope to scoot down on all the streets and through all the alleys, but I would like at least to provide some good snapshots of what is available, and give a sense of its importance. While so doing, I will also take occasional excursions to view the French contribution to the study of Franciscan women, French being, after all, my more native habitat.

Overview of Current Italian Scholarship on Franciscan Medieval Women

Italian studies of female religious life, and I would include Franciscan female religious life, make up a large part of what the eminent Berkeley historian Robert Brentano has called "the beautifully intricate, brilliantly exact, and profoundly thoughtful work of the young ecclesiastical historians for which Italy should now

---

[2]Paul Lachance, OFM, *The Spiritual Journey of the Blessed Angela of Foligno According to the Memorial of Frater A.* (Rome: Studia Antoniana. Cura Pontificii Athenaei Antoniani Edita, N. 29, 1984) and *Angela of Foligno: Complete Works* (Mahwah, NJ: Paulist Press, 1993).

be famous."[3] Unfortunately, this tremendous volume of superb scholarship remains largely unknown outside of Italy in part because relatively few American scholars read Italian, and those who do read it are likely to be frustrated by the peculiarities of Italian academic publishing. Since Italy has a limited market for scholarly books, Italian historians tend to favor the essay or article. Some of the finest scholarship thus receives very limited diffusion—in the published proceedings of one of Italy's frequent conferences, in catalogs of exhibits such as those commemorating Francis of Assisi, Clare of Assisi, and Umbrian holy women.

The Italian propensity, also, for centennial celebrations means that in any given year we are likely to be treated to honor the anniversary of some saint's birth, conversion, death, entrance into a Third Order, or even arrival in a city. I don't know of any that celebrates the departure of a saint from a city! Woe to the librarian caught in the dilemma of how to classify the *atti* of these congresses or to the scholar who tries to look for how they are classified in a library!

Nor is this scholarly production limited to conference papers. Scores, even hundreds of articles have appeared, sometimes in the most obscure and hard to find periodicals. To peruse the periodicals sponsored by the Franciscan family, for instance, is already a daunting task: e.g., *Collectanea Francescana*, *Archivum Franciscanum Historicum*, *Laurentianum*, *Antonianum*, *Analecta*, *T.O.R.*, *Miscellanea Francescana*, *Studi Francescani*. *Italia Francescana*, *La Verna*, *Vita Minorum*, *Forma Sororum*, *Le Venezie Francescane*, *Picenum Seraphicum*. In addition, there are the secular reviews: e.g., *Revista di Storia della Chiesa in Italia*, *Medievo Latina*, *Studi Medievali*, *Mélanges de l'Ecole Française de Rome*. To give you some further idea of the task, if you want to find, for example, an important essay by Roberto Rusconi on "La tradizione manoscritta delle opere degli Spirituali nelle biblioteche dei predicatore e dei conventi dell'Osservanze," you have to find a library that carries *Picenum Seraphicum* published by Italian friars from the Marches and which, I understand, has only recently resumed publication. Or, similarly, if you want Marco Bartoli's

---

[3]Robert Brentano, "Italian Ecclesiastical History: The Sambin Revolution," *Medievalia et Humanistica*, n. 14 (1986): 193.

"Chiara testimone di Francesco," you need to locate the *Quaderni Catanesi di Studi Classici e Medievali*.

While surveying contemporary Italian contributions to the field of Franciscan women, it is important also to be aware of the salient features of current Italian historical scholarship. Even if not as vital as in the past, Italy still has a thriving community of historians who write as committed members of one or another branch of the Franciscan family. Increasingly, however, the banner of Franciscan scholarship is being passed on to lay women and men such as Claudio Leonardi, Ernesto Menesto, Anna Benvenuti Papi, Maria Pia Alberzoni, Roberto Rusconi, Mario Sensi (diocesan priest), Giovanni Miccoli, Marco Bartoli, Chiara Frugoni, Giovanna Casagrande, Felix Accroca (diocesan priest), and Romana Guarnieri. Most of these scholars focus on the intersection of religious, political, economic, and social forces often within carefully circumscribed geographical limits. They found their studies on a thorough and intimate familiarity with rich local manuscript collections, statutes, necrologies, testaments, archives, and civic and chancery registries. Daniel Bornstein has recently observed:

> The hallmark of their work is a rigorous empiricism, a patient, exacting accumulation of precise detail. From these hard edged bits of information, meticulously arranged, an image gradually emerges, an image with acknowledged gaps and blank spaces, but utterly convincing in its overall solidity: a mosaic rather than a sketch.[4]

These historians, furthermore, tend to shy away from grand comparisons and generalizations such as exemplified by the French Annales school (e.g. Vauchez, Le Goff). For someone like Sensi or Zarri, too much precision must be sacrificed, too many inconvenient burrs must be planed smooth, too much empirical truth must be falsified in the pursuit of such global generalizations. Their conviction, rather, is that "the broadest questions demand the most exact answers, and that the only way to arrive at those answers is

---

[4]Daniel Bornstein, "Women and Religion in Late Medieval Italy: History and Historiography," in *Women and Religion in Medieval and Renaissance Italy*, ed. Daniel Bornstein and Roberto Rusconi, trans. Margery J. Schneider (Chicago: The University of Chicago Press, 1996), 13.

through a scrupulously accurate and thorough perusal of the available documentary sources."[5]

Concern, then, with the primary sources is evident not only in the rich footnotes in their books and essays, but in the readiness of Italian scholars to dedicate their energies to the demanding task of editing and publishing texts, documents, and primary sources: e.g., the rich mine of information contained in the *Memoriale di Monteluce* (the chronicles of the Poor Clares of Perugia from 1448 to 1838); the critical editions of the writings of Angela of Foligno, Margaret of Cortona; the canonization trial of Clare of Montefalco.

What Italian scholars perhaps tend to neglect is the devotional or spiritual dimension of history, something which someone of the stature of Roberto Rusconi readily acknowledges. For instance, in the recent *Storia dell'Italia Religiosa* the highly accredited editors consciously avoided giving too much space to mystical and spiritual currents because, they argue, these have been sufficiently studied in the past. As result of this option, Giula Barone's essay on "Gli ordini mendicanti," for instance, mentions Bonaventure's political and educational involvements, but not a word is said of his *Itinerarium* or *Lignum Vitae* and their monumental influence in not only medieval but all of subsequent Christian spirituality.

Are Franciscan Women Making a Difference?

Let us now enter more fully into the question at hand: Are Franciscan women making a difference? It may seem surprising at first glance, but I think you will agree that it is entirely appropriate that we begin to respond to the theme of this conference by starting with Francis, the founder of the movement. Did women make a difference in Francis's life?

The Contribution of Jacques Dalarun

A recent book by Jacques Dalarun—*Francesco: un passaggio. Donna e donne negli scritti e nelle leggende di Francesco d'Assisi* (1994) is written in answer to this question.[6] In *Passagio*, Dalarun makes the

---

[5]Bornstein, 14

[6]Since Dalarun is an important new voice in Franciscan studies, a brief overview of his major works is in order. His first book is *L'impossible sainteté. La vie retrouvé de*

point, one increasingly made by other contemporary scholars, that in the later Middle Ages God changes sex, and religion adopts a feminine face, *se fait femme*. Language itself tumbles and falls as the Latin, the patriarchal language of male clerics, becomes maternal and finds its linguistic expression in the emerging vernacular languages.

The question that Dalarun raises in *Passagio* is the following: Does Francis of Assisi play a role in the changing perception of the role of women and the trend to feminization in the historiography of medieval men and women and, as a consequence of this changed perception, in how the two genders relate to each other? Is Francis then, the source that in some way can explain this changing perception and reversal of roles? Is he the one who makes the passage? How does it play out in him?

In his survey of the role that Francis played in the shift to the feminine, Dalarun focuses on four categories: the real women that Francis encountered—his mother, Clare, and "brother Jacopa; woman in the singular, that is to say the generic image, the ideological construct which medieval writers conceived to be the essence of the feminine, and this with the help of the great figures of Scripture and Tradition from Eve to Mary; the feminine, that is to say the allegories—elements, virtues, institutions which are clearly represented in the feminine mode such as lady poverty, sister water, sister mother earth; finally, the category of feminization—all the shifts and the transgressions wherein a man is represented as having clearly feminine traits or roles.

Women and Feminization in the Writings of Francis

In the known writings of Francis, the twenty-nine texts, who are the women mentioned and how many times? The answer is clear and simple. None and never. To be sure he addressed himself three times, but collectively, to real women—Clare and her sisters in

---

Robert d'Arbrissel (1985). (Robert d'Arbrissel was the founder of the double monastery of Fontevrault.) Dalarun's second book is *La sainte et la cité*. *Micheline de Pesaro (?1356), Tertiaire Franciscaine*, (1992). His other major book is entitled " *Lapsus Linguae*": *La Légende de Claire de Rimini*, (1994), adding another name to the chorus of Franciscan women's voices neglected until very recently. Dalarun's most recent effort is *La Malaventura di Francesco d'Assisi; Per un uno storico delle leggende Francescane (1996)*. This book is a critical overview of the early hagiographical literature surrounding Francis. Lastly, we note his work *Chiara e la diffusione delle clarisse nel secolo XIII*.

chapter six of the Rule of Clare and in the Canticle of Exhortation to Clare and the Poor Ladies, referring to them as "my ladies," and "little poor ones." Strangely enough, in the second Admonition, the one concerning the Fall and the nature of original sin, Adam is mentioned but not Eve. This is quite striking given the fact that in the patristic and monastic tradition prevalent at the time, Eve carries the heavy share of the burden for the fall of humanity.

Dalarun points out that Francis's thought also reflects the mysogyny of the times. In both Rules he sets up clear and severe warnings concerning the frequentation of women. In the *Regula non bullata*, with rare violence, he calls upon the fraternity to abandon totally and chase away any brother guilty of fornication.

As for the Virgin Mary, she appears fourteen times in Francis's writings. Dalarun, basing himself largely on the work of Optatus Von Asseldonk and aside from the traditional titles attributed to Mary, underlines the quite original title of Mary in her relationship with the Trinity, in particular as spouse of the Holy Spirit, and the quite Franciscan emphasis on Mary as the one who chose poverty in order to receive in her womb the Word made flesh. Finally, aside from Martha and Mary as *exempla* for life in the hermitages, no other woman saint is mentioned in Francis's writings.

So, Dalarun argues, it is not so much real women that carry a positive view of the feminine for Francis but rather feminine figures and allegories—the courtly service that must be rendered to Mary, the lady, the holy Queen; our lady holy poverty; and, finally, the Poor Ladies, the "little poor ones" who have the duty to incarnate the Marian ideal that the allegory of dispossession represents.

What is most striking, then, in Francis's writings, according to the French scholar, is the gender reversal and the growing feminization of his spiritual vision. The bond that Francis wishes to establish for the fraternity is a brotherly love that is maternal: "brothers are to love and care for one another as a mother nourishes her son." In the hermitages "two are to serve as mothers" and "the two others as sons." And to console Brother Leo, Francis writes: "I tell you this, my son as a mother." According to Dalarun, then, "To be woman, more precisely to be mother" for Francis "is the most eloquent way to define his conception of the government of the order."[7]

An even more telling evidence of the feminization of Francis's spiritual vision occurs in the Letter to the Faithful where he describes the effects received by those who do penance in the Franciscan way:

> They will be the children of the heavenly Father whose works they do. And they are spouses, brothers, and mothers of our Lord Jesus Christ. We are spouses when the faithful soul is joined to Jesus Christ by the Holy Spirit. We are brothers when we do the will of his Father who is in heaven. We are mothers when we carry him in our heart and body through love and a pure and sincere conscience, we give birth to him through his holy manner of working, which should shine before others as an example (2Ep Fid 49-53).

Even if Francis doesn't elaborate on them, to be noted here are the traditional mystical themes of being espoused to Christ, divine filiation, and the birth of Christ in the soul. Or, in other words, as Dalarun observes, the goal is to be "so strongly a son of Jesus the mother that one becomes the mother of the son."[8]

Further elaborating on the fact that for Francis there seems to be little space for real women and yet an intense interest in feminization, Dalarun aptly quotes Caroline Bynum's statement that

> Francis of Assisi and Henry Suso are probably the thirteenth and fourteenth century men whose piety is most "feminine" if we use the term feminine, as historians of spirituality have done, to mean affective, exuberant. lyrical, and filled with images. Man becomes woman metaphorically or symbolically to express his renunciation or loss of male power, authority, and status. He becomes woman as Eckhart said, in order to express his fecundity, his ability to conceive God within.[9]

---

[7]Jacques Dalarun, *François d'Assise: Un Passage*, tr. Catherine Dalarun-Mitrovistsa (Paris: Actes Sud, 1997), 272-273. Throughout I am quoting from the French edition: The Italian title is *Francesco: Un Passagio: Donna e Donne negli Scritti e nelle Leggende di Francesco d"Assisi* (Rome: Viella, 1994).

[8]Dalarun, 273.

[9]Caroline Walker Bynum, *Holy Feast and Holy Fast: The Religious Significance of Food to Medieval Women* (Berkeley: University of California Press, 1987), 105.

Woman and the Feminine in the Legends

After observing the role of woman and the feminine in the writings, Dalarun, in *Passagio*, reviews the complex dossier of the various legends, the early hagiographical literature surrounding Francis. Among his findings he notes the asymmetry—practically all is about Francis, very little about Clare.

The second life of Celano, for instance, never mentions Clare. If Francis and Clare were a mystical couple and were indissolubly related, this seems, as Dalarun points out, to have escaped the notice of those who knew them best, for they do not mention it. Dalarun even thinks it doubtful that the episode of Clare counseling Francis as to whether he should choose the life of a hermit or of an itinerant preacher is authentic. He thinks that Bonaventure (the only one to record the account) inserted it in his *Legenda major* to buttress his vision of preaching as a primary function of a true Franciscan. As for Francis's relationship to Clare and her community, it is significant that he never calls Clare by her first name, but rather his "Christian Sister," much like he called lepers his "Christian brothers." And he referred to the community at San Damiano as "Poor Ladies" while Clare preferred "Poor Sisters." As for the foundation of San Damiano, from all the evidence (much more than can be noted here), Dalarun concludes that Francis is "not against its formation but doesn't spend much time thinking about it, for the simple reason that for him it was secondary."[10]

Among other findings of *Passagio*, Dalarun notes the paradox that the less the Poverello takes care of real women, the more his own femininity comes to the fore. He also observes that the spiritual success of the early Franciscan movement took place mainly outside the channels of the Order of Clare. It is the penitents, the tertiaries, the recluses, and the beguines who appropriated, in their own way, the extravagant behavior of this "new fool." But here again, Francis himself was not directly the agent, but rather his example provided the impulse and triggered the chain reaction. This later observation concurs with that of another highly esteemed Italian scholar, Claudio Leonardi, in a paper opening the Fourteenth

---

[10]Dalarun, 78.

International Congress of Franciscan Studies on Thirteenth-Century Franciscans and Franciscanism: "Francis's heritage was not passed on to institutions, but was rather perpetuated at the level of mysticism, in a few women such as Angela of Foligno, Clare of Montefalco; a mysticism lived at the personal private level." Leonardi considers St. Francis the "father of this mysticism open to the world."

Clare of Assisi

It is time to leave Francis and take a view of what can be found on another street, scoot down another *strada*: Clare of Assisi, the first Franciscan woman. Highlighting contemporary efforts to bring Franciscan women to the forefront is, certainly, the celebrations and congresses honoring the eighth centenary of Clare's birth. Without making any claim to be complete, I do have some acquaintance with most of the proceedings from Italian congresses held in Assisi, Spoleto, Bari, Rieti, Sabina, Teramo, Rome, and Fara, as well as from French ones in Millau, Beziers, Montpellier, Perpignan, Montreal (Canada).

The most prestigious congress of the centenary was the so-called U.N.E.S.C.O. conference held near Paris and presided over by Cardinal Lustigier.[11] The international array of contributors included Claudio Leonardi, Dominic Rigaux, Nicole Bériou, Mario Sensi, Francis Rapp, Jacques Dalarun, André Vauchez, Danielle Regnier-Bohler, Marco Bartoli, Gabriella Zarri, Marie-Colette Roussey, and Pierre Brunette. A quote from the concluding remarks by Claudio Leonardi provides us with a glimpse of what surfaced: "Clare is no longer eclipsed by Francis. The perspective has changed. One cannot say that Clare is simply the spiritual daughter of Francis. She is his spiritual spouse. And, because of this, it is difficult to decide what belongs to one and what belongs to the other."

So, even if the literature on Clare still pales in comparison to that devoted to Francis, nonetheless, the findings of the various centennial congresses and most recent research challenges put to rest a prevailing hagiographical image of Clare as a colorless,

---

[11]*Sainte Claire d'Assise et sa Posterité*, ed. Geneviève Brunel-Lobrichon, Dominique Dinet, Jacqueline Gréal, Damien Vorreux (Paris: Les Éditions Franciscaines, 1995).

subservient woman, bereft of originality and identity, walking (if not disappearing) in the shadow of Francis as his "little plant." What emerges, rather, is a woman endowed with a powerful spiritual personality, courageous and tenacious in pursuit of her goal to follow "the Christ who was poor and crucified." What is clear, moreover, is that for the first time we are noting not only Clare and Francis's partnership and solidarity as cofounders of the Franciscan movement, but that we are beginning to understand "Francis from the point of view of Clare" (Brunette) and, after Francis's death, Clare as a pillar of the resistance, even as mother of the Spirituals (Flood), the radical wing of the early Franciscan heritage.

Not directly related to the centenary, but relevant to the changing image of Clare, is her portrayal in Liliana Cavani's film, *San Francesco*. If you see the film you will likely be struck by the portrayal of Clare as an attractive young women cavorting in the Umbrian hills with the early companions of Francis, "those who were with him," and telling stories, flashbacks of their remembrance of him after his death. Cavani's portrayal is obviously a considerable adjustment of the historical facts. In an interview, she explained her reconstruction:

> From childhood on, my imagination has been filled with trying to understand who Clare was. The intention of the film is to rebuild an image of Clare which is not bound to an historical reconstruction of who she was but a projection of what she can be imagined, a cinematic transcodification, a symbolic recreation at the existential level. For me Clare was an intellectual, a creative personality, a woman who elaborated a personal vision and sharing in the creative process with Francis. She was not a passive follower of Francis but actively and subjectively collaborating with the spiritual project of Francis to the point that if there was a copyright on the Franciscan project both would have to sign it.

Finally, significant among other recent efforts, there are essays on Clare by Werner Maleczek (published in German in *Collectanea Francescana* and now in *Greyfriars*),[12] questioning the authenticity of

---

[12]The original Maleczek publication was entitled *Das "Privilegium Paupertatis" Innocenz III Und das Testament der Klara von Assisi Uberlegungenzur Frage ihrer Echtheit*, published in Rome in 1995 by the Capuchin Istituto Storico. An English

Clare's Testament and even the privilege of poverty granted by Innocent III. There are also articles by Optatus van Asseldonk, "Sorores minores una nuova impostazione del problema" and Giovana Casagranda, "Presenza di Chiara in Umbria nei secoli XIII-XIV." Maria Pia Alberzoni, another emerging Franciscan scholar, has published a book entitled *Chiara e il Papato*.[13] She has also written a good summary of contemporary research on Clare entitled "Chiara di Assisi e il francescanesimo feminile" in *Francesco d'Assisi e il primo secolo di storia francescana*. This book is the most recent significant attempt to write a complete and synthetic history of the early Franciscans since Gratien de Paris's fragmented and dated *L'histoire de la fondation et de l'évolution de l'Ordre des frères mineurs*. Another important essay in *Francesco d'Assisi e il primo secolo* which falls into the framework of the theme of the present conference is Giovanna Casgrande's "Un ordine per i laici: Penitenza e Penitenti nel Duecento." Each of the essays in *Francesco d'Assisi e il primo secolo* contains excellent bibliographies.

One final remark on contemporary Clare research. What to my mind is still missing is a more thorough study of Clare as a mystic. To be sure there have been valiant efforts in this regard. I mention specifically those essays by Jean Leclerc[14] and Ingrid Peterson[15] published in *Greyfriars*, as well as those by the Capuchin Frederic Raurel, in *Collectanea Francescana* and elsewhere, linking Clare's nuptial mysticism with its forerunners in the Cistercian commentaries of the Song of Songs. But I for one would like to see more said on what indeed Clare did experience "in the wine cellar with the left hand of the heavenly spouse under her head and his right hand embracing her with the happiest kisses of his mouth!"

---

translation appears as "Questions about the Authenticity of the Privilege of Poverty of Innocent III and of the Testament of Clare of Assisi," tr. Cyprian Rosen, OFM Cap. and Dawn Nothwehr, OSF, *Greyfriars Review*, Supplement, 12 (1998): 1-80.

[13]Maria Pia Alberzoni, *Chiara e Il Papato* (Milan: Edizioni Biblioteca Francescana, 1995). For an English work on the topic by Alberzoni see *Greyfriars* issue noted immediately above.

[14]Jean Leclerq, "St. Clare and Nuptial Spirituality," *Greyfriars. Review*, 10.2 (1996): 171-78.

[15]Ingrid Peterson, OSF, "Clare of Assisi's Mysticism of the Poor Crucified," *Greyfriars Review*, 9.2 (1995): 163-92.

Clare's Posterity

So much remains to be done on Clare's posterity. Among the many questions—by whom was Clare's rule adopted and how was it followed? The U.N.E.S.C.O. congress was one of the few during the centenary celebrations that devoted much attention to the *mulieres fortes* that followed her example.[16] Marie-Colette Roussey's paper, "An Atlas of Poor Clare Monasteries. Stages in the Geographic Expansion," provided a good framework for further studies. Elisabeth Lopez gave an excellent presentation on Colette of Corbie She notes that if Clare was the first women to write a rule for consecrated religious women, Colette is the first woman to reform the Second Order, some seventeen monasteries under her aegis. Part of the originality of her reformation program, even if the attempt was short-lived, was to create a men's order at the service of the Clares. Francis Rapp presented an excellent paper on the Reformation Poor Clare, Caritas Pirckheimer. For decades, he observes, the community under her leadership survived the harassment of the Protestant Reformers of Neuremberg, remaining steadfast in their resistance and in absolute fidelity to Clare's ideal—and this without the availability of the Eucharist and preaching.

A very useful text for the study of Poor Clare life and mystics is *Le sante vive: Cultura e religiosità femminile nella prima eta moderna* by Gabriella Zarri (also among the presenters in Paris).[17] In it Zarri, among the foremost of a new wave of Italian scholars, discusses both the early-modern model of women's sainthood and the political and social functions carried out by the women mystics. Here is how Zarri summarizes her findings:

> Whoever considers female religious life in the fifteenth and sixteenth centuries cannot help but be struck by the devotion and learning of the Franciscan second order nuns. Significantly, it was the female branch that supplied the Franciscan movement with that devout vernacular literature which the male branch produced in minimal quantities" since the Franciscan friars concerned themselves above all

---

[16]*Sainte Claire d'Assise et sa Postérité, VIII Centenaire de Sainte Claire: Actes du colloque de l'UNESCO* (Paris, Les Éditions Franciscaines, 1995).

[17]Gabriella Zarri, *Le sante vive: Cultura e religiosità femminile nella prima eta moderna* (Torino, 1990).

with works of immediate utility to their own pastoral
activities, in particular, preaching to the laity in the
vernacular and hearing the confessions of the faithful.[18]

Zarri further comments:

Belonging to the nobility, educated, authors of devotional
texts of noteworthy literary and spiritual value, the Poor
Clares who lived between the fifteenth and sixteenth
centuries represent perhaps the most advanced point or
best referent for the religious literature produced during
this period.[19]

The two most significant works which Zarri mentions are
Catherine of Bologna's (or de Vigri's) *Seven Spiritual Weapons* and
Battista da Varano's *The Mental Sorrows of Christ in his Passion*. Both
Catherine and Battista were early Renaisance women visionaries who
shared a courtly and humanistic formation, an initial mighty battle to
extricate themselves from their cultural and familial bonding in order
to obey a call to enter a strict Poor Clare life, an intense love of the
suffering Christ and desire to suffer the evil that had befallen him,
("il mal patire," to use an expression, difficult to translate, which
Battista often used in her writings and which she likely borrowed
from Catherine.) Both also eventually became abbesses of their
respective monasteries, but they are especially remembered because
they were exceptionally gifted writers, virtuosos in the description of
the art of spiritual combat and mystical experience. Catherine was
also a calligrapher and miniaturist.

One cannot review the major figures of Clare's posterity without
mentioning the "terrible" Veronica Giuliani and her immense
literary production. Her diary, autobiographical writings, letters, and
poetry total twenty-two thousand pages! These have been published
by the Capuchin Institute in Rome under the editorship of the late
Lazaro Iriate.[20] "More suffering! More suffering!" is Veronica's
rallying cry. There are some attempts here and there, but a good
comprehensive study of Veronica's corpus remains to be written.

---

[18]Zarri, 40.

[19]Zarri, 20-21.

[20]*Diario di S. Veronica Giuliani*, Vol. VII, ed. Lazaro Iriarte, OFM Cap. (Assisi:
Ediziioni Porziuncola, 1991).

Franciscan Medieval Lay Women

Contemporary Italian research on Franciscan women is not dedicated exclusively to the Second Order. Its scope is much wider. Until recently the most significant study devoted to the remarkable female presence in medieval religious culture had been Herbert Grundmann's magisterial *Religious Movements in the Middle Ages*, just recently made available in English translation.[21] Caroline Bynum qualified Grundmann's book as "the most important work on twelfth and thirteenth century religion in the past fifty years."[22] In this compelling work of synthesis, Grundman argued that the vibrant and variegated religious developments of the twelfth and thirteenth centuries were all part of a single vast religious movement, which took on many forms but all springing from a single impulse—the desire to restore the primacy of apostolic poverty and evangelical preaching. Women shared equally with men in this spiritual awakening. Indeed, their prominent involvement in all its aspects characterized the religious revival of the twelfth and the thirteenth century. More recent research (e.g. by Mario Sensi and Romana Guarnieri) has uncovered that the striking growth of the Beguine movement was not peculiar to the northern corner of Europe, but was continental in scope, including having a strong foothold in Italy.

In the last two decades, studies of medieval religious women, what Caroline Bynum refers to as "the first women's movement," have proliferated. Italy, for one, has hosted a number of major conferences devoted to this theme among the Franciscans. Among other congresses are: *Movimento religioso femminile e francescanesimo nel secolo XIII* (1979); *Il movimento religioso femminile in Umbria nei secoli XIII-XIV* (1982); *La Beata Angelina da Montegiove e il movimento del Terz'Ordine francescano femminile* (1984); *Santa Chiara da Montefalco e il suo tempo* (1981): *La spiritualità di S. Chiara da Montefalco* (1985); *Temi e problemi nella mistica femminile trecentesca* (1983). The latter includes essays on Margherite of Cortona by Enrico Menestò and the iconography of visions by Chiara Frugoni. Frugoni is another important new voice in Franciscan studies, not

---

[21]Tr. Steven Rowan (Notre Dame University Press, 1995).
[22]Caroline Walker Bynum, *Jesus as Mother: Studies in the Spirituality of the High Middle Ages* (Berkeley: U. of California Press, 1982), 4.

only because of her numerous interventions on the rapport between visions and iconography, but notably because of her book, a current bombshell, *Francesco e l'invenzione delle stigmate*.[23] In it she claims that the interpretation of the vision at La Verna as a vision of Christ was a later elaboration promoted by the Order and the curia and extraneous to Francis and his mental outlook. Frugoni has also written a biography of Francis, *Vita di un uomo : Francesco d'Assisi*, which has received wide acclaim and is soon to be available in English.[24]

André Vauchez's book, *Sainthood in the Late Middle Ages*, now also available in English, is another crucial contribution to current French-Italian research on Franciscan medieval lay women.[25] In this monumental analysis of late medieval canonization proceedings, Vauchez gives great prominence to the question of female sanctity. Some of the findings and further research on this theme can also be found in his essay, "The Laity in the Middle Ages: Female Sanctity in the Franciscan Movement." It is included in his book *The Laity in the Middle Ages* which the University of Notre Dame Press published in 1993. Vauchez notes that half of the women subjected to a canonization trial between 1198 and 1431 were connected with the Franciscan spiritual current. He further observes that among those who associated themselves more or less with this current, two tendencies can be noted. One was characterized by a gospel life lived in proximity to and at the service of the poor. St. Elisabeth of Hungary is the one who best exemplifies this ideal. Another and even more important tendency shifted the emphasis from service to the poor, (even though this was usually present) to individual asceticism and contemplation. Umiliana dei Cerchi, Douceline of Aix en Provence, Clare of Montefalco, Rose of Viterbo, Margaret of Cortona, Angela of Foligno, and countless others shared this ideal.

Scrittici mistiche italiane, edited by Giovanni Pozzi and Claudio Leonardi, is another important reference for Italian Franciscan women. It contains good introductions and individual bibliographies, as well as a brief selection from the writings of many Italian women mystics; thirteen out of forty-eight are Franciscan. Also included are

---

[23]Chiara Frugoni, *Francesco e l'invenzione delle stimmate* (Torino: Giulio Einaudi, 1993).

[24]Chiara Frugoni, *Francis of Assisi: A Life* (New York: Continuum, 1998).

[25]André Vauchez, *Sainthood in the Later Middle Ages*, trans. Jean Birrell (Cambridge University Press, 1997).

two essays by the editors. The first of these, Pozzi's "L'alfabeto delle sante," is a valuable introduction to women's mysticism in the Italian context, focusing on the peculiarities of women's mystical discourse. The second introductory essay, Leonardi's "La santita delle donne," is a chronological overview of the history and hagiography of Italian women mystics. Finally, among other helpful resources, are the invaluable *Bibliographia Francescana* in *Collectanea Francescana*, the forty-three volumes (incomplete) of the *Dizionario biografico degli Italiani*, the *Dizionnario degli Instituti di Perfezione*, and the *Bibiotheca Sanctorum*.

Na Prous Boneta and Margaret of Cortona: New Studies

Na Prous Boneta, for one, has suddenly become popular. Na Prous was a Franciscan Tertiary or French Beguine. In 1325, when she was twenty-eight years old, she was tried, condemned as a heretic, and burned at the stake in Carcasson. In 1305, on or about the feast honoring her mentor Peter Olivi, Na Prous was told in a vision that when she had made a vow of virginity some nine months previous, she had been conceived in the Spirit in a reprise of the immaculate conception since all her sins had been forgiven just as Mary's were in her mother's womb. Around 1321, while attending Mass in a Franciscan Church on Good Friday, she saw God's divinity, conversed with each of the persons of the Trinity, and concluded that, as Mary had been a donatrix of the Son, she (Na Prous) had been designated as a donatrix of the Holy Spirit. It had also been revealed to her that Pope John XXII was the Antichrist and Thomas Aquinas was the new Cain. Furthermore, according to the new dispensation of the Spirit, the sacraments had lost their power. To be saved one must believe both Olivi and herself. What is very unique about Na Prous is that she is a rare case of a women heading a resistance movement. Her house became a refuge for the underground railroad at the service of persecuted Franciscan Spirituals. Na Prous is the subject of recent essays by David Burr[26]

---

[26]David Burr, "Na Prous Boneta and Olivi," *Collectanea Francescana*, 67.3-4 (1997): 477-500.

and Barbara Newman.[27] Louisa Burnham of Northwestern University is presently doing doctoral work on her.

Margaret of Cortona is another emerging star on the Franciscan horizon. Fortunato Iozelli, an Italian Franciscan, has just published a new critical edition of Margaret's biography by Giunta Bevegnati.[28] The edition contains an excellent introduction. Among Jozelli's conclusions: "There is no doubt," he asserts, "that Beveganati was inspired by classic models of hagiography in writing his biography. Its purpose is to edify and not to obey the canons of strictly historical research." The emphasis, Jozelli advances, is on Margaret's interior life, highlighting the presence of auditions, visions, and raptures. Every Friday, for instance, the citizens of Cortona would gather in the Franciscan church to witness Margaret, a "new Mary Magdelene," bodily reenact the passion of Christ. Finally, Jozelli notes, the purpose of the biography is to provide a religious program for the laity, which includes "sharing the condition of the poor and promoting peace initiatives." Thomas Renna, no stranger to the Medieval Congress at Kalamazoo but a welcome newcomer to Franciscan studies, is presently doing research on Margaret and has been contracted to translate her biography by the Franciscan Institute of St. Bonaventure University.

Angela of Foligno

In 1935, in spite of a plethora of already existing editions and translations, M. J. Férré, in his own edition and French translation, could still present Angela of Foligno as a "too little known great mystic of the fourteenth century." In these past ten years, however, there has been an avalanche of essays, books, translations, and congresses about the figure and the work of this blessed Franciscan tertiary. Angela has moved up to the front ranks of medieval feminine sanctity, "one of four female medieval evangelists" to use the very recent accolade given to her by Bernard McGinn (the other

---

[27]Barbara Newman, *From Virile Woman to Woman-Christ* (Philadelphia, University of Pennsylvania Press, 1995), ch. 6.

[28]Iunctae Bevegnatis, *Legenda de Vita et Miraculis Beatae Margaritae de Cortona*, ed. Fortunato Iozelli, OFM (Grottaferrata, Rome: Bibliotheca Franciscana Ascetica Medii Aevi, Tom. XIII, 1997).

three being Marguerite Porete, Mechthild of Magdeburg, and Hadewijch).[29]

Among the recent initiatives propelling Angela to the forefront of contemporary awareness are: a new critical edition of her writings; two major congresses in Foligno, one in 1985 honoring the seventh centenary of her conversion and another in 1991 honoring her entrance in the Franciscan Third Order; a round-table discussion entitled "E esistita Angela da Foligno?" held in Rome in 1995, whose proceedings have yet to be published; an inconographic inventory first exhibited in Foligno then published in *Sante e Beate Umbre fra il XII e XIV secolo* (1986); a *Centro documentazione beata Angela* whose goal is to assemble all existing writings, documentation, and iconography about her; a *Cenacolo della beata Angela*, whose purpose is to promote awareness and the cult of Angela on the local, national, and international level; new translations of her writings, in Spanish, in French, and two in Italian, one complete and the other partial; an introduction and English translation in the prestigious Classics of Western Spirituality series, now over 4,000 copies sold; a French version, close to a thousand sold; my thesis, some six hundred copies sold; a number of biographies and book length studies, four in Italian, three in French, including a very recent one (1998), likely a best seller, by a well known French writer Michel Casenave; a regularly updated complete bibliography by Sergio Andreoli of Foligno; countless essays, theses, and presentations, including, for instance, five papers on her sponsored by the Franciscan Federation at the recent International Medieval Congress in Kalamazoo; a film in preparation directed by Enrico Bellani, a disciple of the great Italian director Michelangelo Antonioni; and a committee working on her canonization and proclamation as a doctor of the church. Finally, she is the only mystic, in my acquaintance, whose complete writings are available on the world wide web, which even includes a chat box inviting contributions and comments!

---

[29]Bernard McGinn, *The Flowering of Mysticism: Men and Women in the New Mysticism—1200-1350* (New York: Crossroad, 1998), 141.

More on Angela's Influence

Like many other mystic texts, Angela's book belongs to the highly suspect corners of history. Mystical narratives are like family secrets that one wants to know but is afraid that they will come out in the open. They are texts on love which touch wounds, denials, impossible desires, and the basic issues of life. They disconcert and raise questions. They tell us our lives must change. Mystical texts, by their very nature it seems, also travel. The presence of a large number of existing manuscripts and the vast area in which they are found bears out that Angela's writings have been widely read over the centuries.

The journey of Angela's *Liber*, however, is not easy to trace. Its diffusion was underground initially, and it makes its appearance far from its source in sometimes unexpected places. In both the English and the French versions of Angela's book, I have indicated some of the moments in which this hot text bursts into flame. One notable instance, among others, is the discovery that Teresa of Avila, in describing the torments of the sixth dwelling place in her work on *The Interior Castle*, clearly had Angela's text next to her on her writing table. Quite a bit of the language is the same, and the image of "someone hanging, without any support" to describe the agonies of the soul abandoned by God is borrowed directly from Angela. Teresa's oft-quoted line: "I die because I do not die" is, likewise, a direct quote from Angela's seventh supplementary step in the *Memorial*.

A quite recent discovery that I have made on the diffusion of Angela's writings is its use as one of the few books included in the library of sixteenth-century Spanish Franciscan missionaries sent to evangelize the New World (Argentina) by Cardinal Ximenes, an Observant Franciscan. Ximenes was responsible for the first printed edition of Angela's writings, a Latin version in 1505 and a Spanish one in 1510. Angela's story, as a Christian heroine, was used to edify indigenous youth.

Since I cannot hope to cover the entire field, I would like to focus on the more recent influences of Angela's writings in the French-Italian orbit. Surprisingly enough, Angela's writings have been more notably received in France than in Italy. In the French context, she has been read not only in religious circles but outside the ecclesiastical domain among lay readers, in the world of letters and psychoanalysis. This success is due in great part to the French philosopher Ernest Hello's translation, which appeared in 1868. *Le Livre des visions et instructions de la bienheureuse Angèle de Foligno* was enormously successful enjoying as many as ten editions, the most recent one in 1991 by the Editions du Seuil in Paris. What Hello tried to do, as he indicates in his preface, was to translate not according to the letter of the text but according to its spirit: "I tried to bring to life in French what was alive in Latin. I have tried to make the French cry out what the soul cried out in Latin. I have tried to translate tears."

In spite of its many imperfections, some due in part to the fact that he worked from an unreliable manuscript, Hello's brilliant translation catapulted Angela into the consciousness of modern French culture. Countless thousands, both in and out of the Franciscan world, came to know her through it. When it appeared the Protestant Louis Veuillot, for instance, acclaimed its poetic style: "the admirable poetic machine by Dante is no match for the stature and the structure of this poem."[30] The mystic, Elisabeth of the Trinity, quotes her. The novelist George Bernanos, in his *Dialogues des Carmélites*, cites Angela's most noted locution from God: "Ce n'est pas pour rire que je t'ai aimé (My love for you has not been a hoax)!" Teilhard de Chardin will consider Angela as one of his favorite mystics, alongside John of the Cross and Teresa of Avila. Georges Bataille, perhaps, the most important contemporary philosopher to explore the nexus between mysticism and eroticism, frequently refers to Angela in his writings. Still another example of the influence of Hello's version is a play adapted from it by Philipe Clévenot, starring Bérangère Bonvoisin as Angela. *Celle qui ment* is the title of the play, performed in Paris and Rouen in 1984.[31]

Prominent French feminists have also been fascinated with Angela's writings. Simone de Beauvoir, one of the earliest feminist scholars, for instance, refers to Angela in a chapter entitled, "The Mystic," in her book, *The Second Sex*. De Beauvoir sees mysticism in

---

[30]Quoted in *Le livre d'Angèle de Foligno*, tr. Jean-François Godet; ed. T. Matura and P. Lachance (Paris: Jerome Millon, 1995), 42.

[31]Paul Lachance "*Celle qui ment* (The One Who Lies):Angela of Foligno," *Greyfriars Review*, 12.3 (1998): 303-315.

a totally negative light, attributing to it a sadomasochistic character. She concludes her discussion of mystics, which includes Angela, by inviting women to free themselves of any mystical tendencies through "positive action into human history."

Another contemporary French feminist, Luce Irigary, presents mysticism in a more positive light. In one of her books, *Speculum of the Other Woman*, she dedicates a chapter to mysticism entitled, "La mystérique," a term conflating the two terms mystical and hysterical. The chapter teems with allusions to Angela's writings. Irigary tries to debunk the view of mysticism as a passive state, while seeking to give a new vision of mysticism. For Irigary "[Mystic language] is the only place in the history of the West in which woman speaks and acts so publicly." Moreover, mysticism, she asserts, is a typical feminine phenomenon. Consequently, male mystics are left with the imitation, with the "mimicking" of women. In doing so, men abandon their rationality: "This is the place where 'she'—and in some cases he, if he follows 'her' lead—speaks about the dazzling glare which comes from the source of light that has been logically repressed, about 'subject' and 'Other' flowing out into an embrace of fire that mingles for understanding as an obstacle along the path of jouissance and mistrust for the dry desolation of reason."

The way Irigaray classifies mysticism along gender categories has been criticized by Tiziana Arcangeli in an essay entitled, "Re-reading a Mis-Known and Mis-Read Mystic: Angela da Foligno."[32] Arcangeli argues that "by presenting understanding and reason as male attributes, Iragary falls into the trap of using and reinforcing a somewhat essentialist approach. In fact, most feminists want to do away with that essentialism promoted by patriarchy, that is, labeling women as intuitive, emotional, and imaginative, as well as associating men with reason and rationality." Whether one agrees with Irigary's positions or not, the language that she uses is extremely suggestive, and one can feel Angela's text palpitating beneath her own. For instance: "This (the mystic mind) is the place where consciousness is no longer master, where, to its extreme confusion, it sinks into a dark night that is also fire and flames." Or again, on the

---

[32]While lacking complete information on this publication, I direct the reader to *Annali d'Italianistica:Women Mystic Writers*, ed. Dino Cervigni, 13 (1995), 42-44.

consciousness of the mystic: "Expectant expectancy, absence of project and projections. Unbearable sweetness and bitterness, aridity, dizzy horror before the boundless void."

The psychoanalyst Julia Kristeva is still another French feminist intrigued by Angela's writings. In one of her books, *Powers of Horror: An Essay on Abjection*, she makes explicit reference to the shocking passage in the *Memorial* where Angela declares having drunk the pus of the skin of a leper in an advanced state of putrefaction and reports that she and her companion "had tasted its sweetness and it was if we had received Holy Communion." Kristeva comments on this event: "The mystic's familiarity with abjection is a fount of infinite jouissance. One may stress the masochistic economy of the jouissance only if one points out at once that the Christian mystic far from using it to the benefit of a symbolic or institutional power (as happens with dreams, for instance) displaces it indefinitely within a discourse where the subject is reabsorbed (is that a grace?) into communication with the Other and with others. One recalls Francis of Assisi who visited leproseries to give alms and left only after having kissed each leper on the mouth; who stayed with lepers and bathed their wounds, sponging pus and sores. One might also think of Angela of Foligno."

Commenting on the interest in Angela manifested by French feminist and psychoanalytic circles as well as by postmodern thinkers, Cristina Mazzoni, in an essay entitled, "Angela of Foligno and Jacques Lacan," points out that one of the chief characteristics of her writings that makes them so relevant is Angela's "insistence on transgression, on the fact that her language is necessarily a blasphemy—that it goes beyond the accepted and acceptable limits implicitly imposed by religious and cultural discursive conventions regarding the Divine." [33]

Open Warfare on Angela's *Liber*

The brilliant French scholar, the late Michel de Certeau, makes the following observation on the fortunes of mystical texts: "What distinguishes the information that we have on mystical phenomena is

---

[33] *Gender and Text in the Later Middle Ages*, ed. Jane Chance (University Press of Florida), 249.

the fact, a massive one, that they are indissociable from disputes and quarrels. No mysticism without a trial."[34] The first edition of John of the Cross's writings, for instance appeared more than a century after his death and in an incomplete edition eliminating his most daring text, the *Spiritual Canticle*. Nearer to Angela in time, the Beguines, Hadewijch and Marguerite Porete, have only recently been rediscovered, the former towards the end of the last century and the latter towards the middle of this century.

Angela's *Liber*, as already indicated, has had a stormy history, and a secure haven is still far from sight. To the overall neglect which, for the most part, Angela's writings have undergone must also be added the unreliability of the editions. The recent history of the text is full of controversy. It is interesting to note that every new edition dismisses the previous ones as inaccurate. Doncoeur, in his critical edition (1926), states "that the translation of the book of Angela by Hello is totally untrustworthy because it is based on an unreliable work from the sixteenth century." He maintains that his version, his Latin edition and French translation, is "the only pure one." One year later, in 1927, Ferré, disagreeing with Doncoeur's choice of a basic manuscript, published his own edition and translation. Yet, these French scholars do not have the last word on the subject. In their 1985 critical edition, *Il libro della beata Angela da Foligno*, Thier and Calufetti attack Doncoeur's version maintaining that "it cannot be trusted whatsoever." They also critique other previous editions. The Italian edition by Faloci-Pulignani, they point out, "is full of errors." The one by Ferré is "the one with the least errors, but in need of revision."

One would have hoped that the Thier-Calufetti version would have been able to withstand critical appraisal. Not so. Ernesto Menesto, a leading Italian scholar—and he has been joined in his criticism by a host of others—refers to it as an "*occasione mancata*." Another leading scholar, Giovanni Pozzi, in his recent introduction and translation (partial), *Il Libro dell'esperienza* (1992), doesn't even use this critical edition. He considers it as a third "experiment" after the French ones by Doncoeur and Férré. Apparently, it is common for editors of manuscripts to discredit previous editions.

---

[34]"Historicites Mystiques" in *Revue des Sciences Religieuses*, 75 (1985): 330.

Yet, this endless polemic makes the reader suspect that any edition will be outdated in a few years by a supposedly more accurate work.

Did Angela Exist?

The contemporary assault on Angela's book does not limit itself, however, to the quality of its critical editions. *E esitite Angela da Foligno?* was the title of a round table discussion (whose entire proceedings have yet to be published) held in Rome in 1995. The provocative title, "Did Angela Exist?" is taken from that used by a paper given by Jacques Dalarun, the French scholar, whom I have referred to at the very beginning of this present essay. This title, Dalarun notes, is patterned after previous similar French essays: "Did Francis of Assisi Exist?" by Edouard Alençon and "Did St. Louis Exist?" by Jacques Le Goff. Like these authors, Dalarun's purpose is to raise rather fundamental questions on the authorship of the text, on Angela's life, as well as on many other assumptions about her which have until now been unquestioned.

The generally accepted chronology of Angela's story, for instance, has until now been the one established by Férré. Contrary to Férré's presuppositions, Dalarun argues, quite convincingly, that there is no secure basis for dating Angela's birth in 1248; nor can one be too sure of the date of her conversion in 1285; and the date of Angela's entrance into the Third Order in 1291 is a mere supposition. The date of her death, then, on January 4, 1309, is the only sure date available. As for Angela's existence, Dalarun notes that in the rich archives available on Foligno and medieval Italian cities, there is not one mention, not even any allusion, that would indicate her presence during the presumed dates of her life. Furthermore, the name Angela doesn't appear even once in the *Memorial* according to the Assisi codex, the most basic manuscript available. She is referred to throughout the *Memorial* as *quaedam fidelis Christi* ("a certain follower of Christ"); once, however, she is designated by the letter L. Similarly, the *Memorial* doesn't even mention Foligno, only the convent of San Feliciano. One must await the *Instructions* to find Foligno mentioned three times.

Furthermore, Franciscan historians, usually quick to mention the glories of their tradition, are extremely discreet, Dalarun also notes, in regard to Angela. Her name doesn't appear in any known chronicle of the Order until the early fifteenth century: a brief notice in the *De conformitate* of Bartolemeo of Pisa (1401); a mention by Francesco Ximenis (ca. 1409); another mention in a brief poem by a Franciscan tertiary in 1465. The only explicit witness to Angela during this period is a reference to her by Ubertino of Casale in the prologue of his *Arbor Vitae Crucifixae Jesu*, written on Mount La Verna in 1305. For the medieval centuries, Dalarun observes, what keeps Angela's memory alive is neither a biography nor a cult but the transmission of a text in assorted manuscripts—some twenty-eight in the repertory assembled in the fifteenth-sixteenth centuries.

For Dalarun, the *Liber* attributed to Angela is a "mystic fable," a literary and theological fiction composed by a group of Franciscan Spirituals; one of the authors is anonymous and appears in the *Memorial* as *frater A.*, and the other, he suggests, is the flamboyant leader of the Spirituals, Ubertino of Casale. As for the friars who composed the *Instructions*, they are unknown, but many are clearly in the Spiritual camp. At the heart of this fiction, Dalarun concludes, is "the faint echo of a woman who was named or was called Angela, who lived in the Umbrian city of Foligno in the late thirteenth and early fourteenth century and who died 'anno dominice incarnationis MCCCIX pridie nonas januarii.'"

Another important paper at this same Rome conference was given by Romana Guarnieri. Guarnieri is one of the "grandes dames" of European medieval scholarship. Among her many contributions, she is credited with establishing Marguerite Porete as the author of *The Mirror of Simple Souls*. Guarnieri is also the author of the preface in the Angela of Foligno volume in the Classics of Western Spirituality series and a friend. She graciously gave me a copy of her lengthy (sixty-eight pages) and very erudite presentation entitled "Santa Angela?" In it Guarnieri iterates and amplifies many of the positions taken up by Dalarun. Her concern can be summed up in one of her opening salvos: "In brief, who or what are we about to canonize: a woman or a book?" Given the present effort to place Angela on the holy altars, Guarnieri opines that "much more serious historical and philological research is needed before such a judgment can be rendered." Like Dalarun, but more documented, Guarnieri also notes how little data on the historical existence of Angela is available.

Almost half of Guarnieri's presentation is devoted to a detailed analysis of the brief (forty-one lines) epilogue or peroration that accompanies Angela's writings. This little studied text is very revelatory. It even climaxes, according to Guarnieri, the Franciscan Spiritual leanings of the entire *Liber* and its subsequent use in the battle that they were waging with the "community." Guarnieri advances the hypothesis that it was very likely written by a learned Spiritual, conceivably Ubertino of Casale, around the year 1300. The "animal, earthbound, diabolical, and pride-filled teachers" which the text virulently assaults are clearly representatives of the "community" wing who held the rule of Francis to be impracticable *sine glossa* and were convinced of the necessity for studies, large convents, and churches for pastoral activity—and enemies, furthermore, of a poor contemplative life withdrawn in hermitages. Against these "proud, clever, lettered, hypocritical, empty talkers, filled with prudence of the flesh," the polemics continues, "God in his eternal wisdom has raised Angela, a woman, humble, simple, unschooled, condemning and despising herself, zealous in deeds and silent in words, filled with the prudence of the Spirit which is the science of the cross of Christ. Thus, a strong woman brought to light what was buried under by blind men and their worldly speculations."

The epilogue then proceeds to intensify the argument. Much like Francis was referred to by the Spirituals as another Christ (*alter Christus*) and his rule equivalent to the gospel, Angela was given an eschatological and prophetic role. To "fight against Angela" is equivalent to being against "the way of Christ and his teaching." Angela, Guarnieri proposes, according to this epilogue, could even be conceived, as was Francis, as the angel of the third seal of the Book of Revelation. As such, she is introducing the third and final stage of the history of the Church, for she is "the mirror without blemish of God's majesty and image of his kindness" who "makes of all her sons prophets of truth" renewing the last times.

Buttressed by arguments based throughout on Scriptural texts, the final statement of the epilogue further enhances Angela's prophetic role. The text argues that as "the apostles learned of the resurrection from a woman" likewise the rule of Francis "dead in carnal men since the suffering-filled observance of Francis and his companions, has now been rendered immortal by the observance of our holy mother, . . . [and] the gift of prophecy has been transmitted to the female sex to shame men who are doctors of the law but who transgress the commandments of God."

Finally, along with Dalarun and also Mario Sensi, Guarnieri advances the hypothesis that Ubertino of Casale is not only the author of the epilogue, but is also one of the anonymous readers mentioned in the *Liber* who have read Angela's text, even discussed it with her, and made it known to the champion of the spirituals, Cardinal Colonna, whose name appears in most codices in the Prologue of the *Liber* but is scratched off significantly in the Assisi codex.

Obviously, there is more light needed on Angela's *Liber*, which, Guarnieri advances, is likely "the most extraordinary and fascinating mystical text in the history of Christian mystical literature." It [Angela+collaborators and/or the *Liber*?], to quote again from the epilogue, "has no match on earth."

Franciscan Women Mystics

Even if Angela can be qualified as the greatest Franciscan women mystic, she is not the only one in the rich mystical tradition of the followers of the Poverello and Clare. There are many others whose names are, much to our embarrassment, unknown to us. A list of some of them is provided by a projected ten-volume history of Franciscan mysticism, *I Mistici Francescani*, whose second volume has just been published. The list is as follows. fourteenth century: Angela of Foligno; fifteenth: Colette of Corbie, Caterina Vigri of Bologna, Eustochia Calafato, Caterina of Genoa; sixteenth: Anna d. Croce Pons de Leon, Camilla Battista da Varano; seventeenth: Giacinta Marescotti, Maria di Gesu d'Agreda, Maria Domitilla Galluzzi (a little known stigmatic nun from Lombardy whom E. Ann Matter has wrtten about);[35] eighteenth: Veronica Giuliani, Maria

---

[35]E. Ann Matter, "Interior Maps of an Eternal External: The Spiritual Rhetoric of Maria Domitilla Galluzzi d'Acqui" in *Maps of Flesh and Light: the Religious Experience of Medieval Women Mystics*, ed. Ulrike Wiethaus (Syracuse, NY: Syracuse U. Press, 1993), 61-73.

Maddalena Martinengo, Francesca Guiseppina de Castillo, Chiara Isabella Fornari, Maria Nazarena Sandri, Diomira Serri del Verbo Incarnato, Maria della Natività, Chiara Isabella Gherzi; nineteenth: Maria di S. Tommaso de Villeneuve, Maria Annunziata Hermoso de Mendoza, Elisabetta del SS Sacramento, Marie-Colette du Sacré Coeur; twentieth: Maria degli Angeli Sorazu, Maria Margherita Cainni, Eve Lavalière, Speranza di S. Raffaele, Maria Costanza Panas, Maria Veronica del SS Sacramento, Giovanna Francesca dello Spirito Santo, Maria della Trinità.

We are all looking for words that induce a departure, stories that inspire us, give us staying power, a bed to rest on, a place to get lost—and for this we do well to listen to the great heroines of our tradition.

Women and Franciscan Studies:
The State of the Question

Margaret Carney, OSF

In 1994 Kenan Osborne, OFM, invited me to prepare an essay on women's contribution to Franciscan theology for the volume ultimately published by the Franciscan Institute entitled *The History of Franciscan Theology.*[1] In that essay I explained why it was impossible to single out women as leaders in the various epochs of theological development and went on to suggest some changes that will help the Franciscan family to remedy this situation in the next millennium. Four years later another collection of studies addresses this topic in the present tense: What difference are women making today to the study of Franciscan theology, history, and philosophy?

As I engaged in conversations with the organizers of this symposium and with my respondents, Roberta A. McKelvie, OSF, and Elise Saggau, OSF, it occurred to me that we tend to stress a common but limited understanding of the term "Franciscan studies." Our talk returned in almost circular fashion to a few indicators, especially the recent emergence of a small number of women with doctoral degrees in Franciscan specializations. The more I pondered the evidence we referenced as signs of progress, the more concerned I became that we might find ourselves in two blind alleys. The first is the tendency to define Franciscan studies in too narrow a sense, thus risking oversight of many scholarly contributions that should occur in a complete catalog of Franciscan scholarship. The second is the temptation to ignore the fact that the recent emergence of a small group of women generally recognized as Franciscan scholars was made possible by the action of earlier generations of American Franciscan women. These women quietly—and, perhaps at times, unwittingly—laid the foundation for those of us who answer the call to scholarly pursuits today

We can turn to our first temptation to begin our discussion. I would like to propose the following approach. Let us consider Franciscan studies as a wide range of disciplines involved in learning

---

[1]*The History of Franciscan Theology*, ed. Kenan B. Osborne, OFM (St. Bonaventure, NY: The Franciscan Institute, 1994).

about the origins, tradition, and development of the Franciscan movement. Philosophy, theology, history, and spirituality play a prominent role, but other disciplines should be included in a comprehensive listing. As a method of determining what can be included in the term Franciscan studies, I believe that we should accept the categories of the *Bibliographia Francescana*, which annually provides notice of all published works pertaining to Franciscan scholarship.[2] The ten divisions that marshal the works of hundreds of contributors year by year include numerous sub-divisions. The entire range of possible approaches to Franciscan studies is really astounding seen from this vantage point. I have included a summary version of these categories in the Appendix to this paper. If the work of every woman scholar who has studied a Franciscan topic in any of these categories was to be listed, I suspect that our "honor roll" would grow much faster than we originally imagined possible.

Those Who Have Gone Before Us

Margaret Oliphant, a prolific nineteenth-century writer of fiction and history, published *Francis of Assisi* in 1870 in England, twenty-three years before Sabatier's biography of the saint.[3] Oliphant tells her readers in the Introduction that she based her research on the sources preserved by the Bollandists in the *Acta Sanctorum*. She describes the importance of Celano's *First Life*, the *Legend of the Three Companions* and the *Legenda* of Bonaventure. She utilized the *Fioretti*, convinced of its value to the tradition by the affection with which the Italian people transmitted it. She describes her debt to the painstaking scholarship of Father Suyskens who worked with Luke Wadding's compilation and acknowledges studies by Karl Hase and Ozanam. She sternly warns her readers—most likely Anglicans who feared any form of Roman Catholic excess—of the dangers of those "biographies (of the Order) which

---

[2]The *Bibliographia Franciscana* is published as a supplement to *Collectanea Francescana* by the Capuchin Historical Institute at Collegio San Lorenzo in Rome. It has been issued separately since 1944 and is the most complete bibliographic tool for Franciscan studies.

[3]Margaret Oliphant, *Francis of Assisi* 1870 (London: Macmillan and Co., Ltd., 1907). For additional information about Mrs. Oliphant, consult *The Cambridge Bibliography of English Literature*, Vol. 3, 1800-1900, 500-501.

sought to raise its founder to the highest fabulous rank of sainthood, or rather of semi-deity."[4] The work went into *thirteen reprints* between its appearance and the year 1907. Few would argue the preeminent claims for Sabatier's distinction as the first modern biographer of the saint.[5] However, should we not take a moment to ponder the fact that this scholarly effort by a Victorian woman has gone unnoticed in the endless chronicles of "the Franciscan Question"?

Strong academic support for research into Franciscan history accounts for several works from Britain: In 1926 Anne Claudine Bourdillon published *The Order of Minoresses in England*.[6] In 1929 Margaret R. Toynbee published her work on St. Louis of Toulouse.[7] Decima L. Douie presented *The Nature and the Effect of the Heresy of the Fraticelli* in 1932. The name of A. G. Little invariably appears in the acknowledgments of these women, testimony to his influence over a generation of British Franciscanists.

The closer we get to our own times, the more likely we are to recognize names that are familiar to the current generation of students. Let us cite just two: Nesta de Robeck and Rosalind Brooke. While de Robeck's work was published before the renaissance of Franciscan studies after the Second Vatican Council, one stands in awe of her careful use of sources and the thorough nature of her biographies. Nor should we forget that her little volume, *St. Clare of Assisi*, actually provided readers with an early English translation of several important sources.[8] It would be thirty years before the scholarly work of Regis Armstrong, OFM Cap., would put these same sources into the hands of students and Franciscans on a massive scale.

---

[4]Oliphant, xv.

[5]See, for example, C. N. L. Brooke, "Paul Sabatier and Saint Francis," *St. Francis of Assisi: Essays in Commemoration, 1982*, ed. Maurice W. Sheehan, OFM Cap. (St. Bonaventure, NY: The Franciscan Institute, 1982).

[6]A. F. C. Bourdillon, *The Order of Minoresses in England* (Manchester: The University Press, 1926).

[7]Margaret R. Toynbee, *S. Louis of Toulouse and the Process of Canonization in the Fourteenth Century* (Manchester: The University Press, 1929).

[8]Nesta de Robeck, *St. Clare of Assisi* (Milwaukee: The Bruce Publishing Co., 1951). Her appendices include The Office of the Passion, The Rule, The Testament, The Cause of Canonization, The Bull of Canonization.

Rosalind Brooke, in the preface to *Early Franciscan Government*,[9] prettily thanks her equally famous husband, Christopher, for taking more than his share of household work so that she could finish her research. This detail is included along with her thanks to such luminaries as Franciscans Michael Bihl and Willibrord-Christian Van Dijk and Benedictine David Knowles. Her acknowledgment of the problems of combining childcare and chores in the kitchen with first-class historical research should give many a woman among us heart. We are grateful for the incisive analysis of this scholar who remained for a very long time one of the few women authorities in our field. In addition to the title mentioned above, her contributions include *The Coming of the Friars* and *Scripta Leonis*.[10] She also contributed many articles and chapters to other volumes.

In concluding this consideration we remind ourselves not to ignore the many essays in various journals and papers delivered at academic congresses by women medievalists. There actually is a large number of female scholars who provide research for our consideration. But to begin a litany or pause for too many illustrations of this "outer circle" will take us too far afield for our purposes.

Foundations of Women's Contributions

Today there are women serving as full-time faculty members at graduate schools of Franciscan theology. This signifies a new expression of commitment by women to the academic pursuit of Franciscan studies. Recent doctoral research by several women has broken new ground in our retrieval of women's history and women's perspectives in theological reflection. Franciscan institutes of higher learning sponsored by women's congregations are innovating in curriculum design and co-curricular initiatives that will offer the

---

[9]Rosalind B. Brooke, *Early Franciscan Government: Elias to Bonaventure* (Cambridge: The University Press, 1959), see p. x.

[10]Rosalind B. Brooke, *The Coming of the Friars* (New York: Barnes & Noble Books, 1975). Brooke begins her Author's Note to this volume with a quote from Winnie the Pooh. It is safe to wager that no other Franciscan scholar to date has cited this source, a favorite of children and probably well known by this working mother. *Scripta Leonis, Rufini et Angeli Sociorum S. Francisci.* ed. and trans. Rosalind B. Brooke (Oxford: Clarendon Press, 1970).

tradition's riches to students. [11]There has even been a slight increase in the number of women in Franciscan congregations who are devoting themselves to serious academic work in various areas of concern to us.

We might note that all of this defies the laws of institutional gravity. It is happening at a time when religious congregations— traditionally the bastions of higher education for Catholic women— face declining numbers of younger (read "student age") women and restricted resources for graduate and doctoral study. The new interest in academic pursuit of Franciscan studies also comes in a season that might be described as inhospitable to such pursuits. The work of the Brookland Commission on women religious and intellectual life offers an important context for this present symposium.[12] Increasing numbers of lay women are now engaged in Franciscan studies in spite of the fact that willingness to embrace such seraphic specialization might not always appear a prudent career choice in today's academy, even in church-related colleges. I am often reminded of the fisherman who encountered me one afternoon years ago on the riverbank behind our campus. My head was buried in my big red Omnibus. He struck up a conversation as he loaded his gear into a nearby truck. After I explained my mysterious major to him he exclaimed: "Oh, lady, get yourself into something where you can make a little money. That stuff won't get you nowhere!"

Given such warnings of lack of financial rewards, paucity of places on small faculties, and the nagging suspicion that we might be escaping the urgent demands of social ministries, we might still ask just what has made it possible for this new growth of women's presence to occur. Let us examine the structures and initiatives that prepared the way for this development in our country for decades prior to Vatican II. At the outset I admit that my focus is on

---

[11]For some examples of this kind of work, the proceedings of meetings of leaders of Franciscan colleges and universities will serve well. For example, see the symposium publication, *Franciscan Charism and Higher Education: Selected Resources for Study*, ed. Kathleen Moffatt, OSF (Aston, Pa.: Sisters of St. Francis, 1990) and *The Franciscan Charism in Higher Education*, ed. Roberta A. McKelvie, OSF, Spirit and Life Series, vol. 2 (St. Bonaventure, NY: The Franciscan Institute, 1992).

[12]This commission began to study the impact of post-counciliar change upon the pursuit of higher studies among women religious in North America in 1988. For detailed information on the research conducted and the 1992 Brookland Conference, see *Women Religious and the Intellectual Life: The North American Achievement*, ed. Bridget Puzon, OSU (Bethesda, MD.: International Scholars Publications, 1996).

developments that took place among women religious. Since it is from the ranks of the sisters that the first wave of Franciscan scholarship emerged in this country, I believe that this approach is valid. Future studies will undoubtedly see a major shift taking place within this decade, but that will be someone else's task to record.

I wish to identify some of the programs and organizations that laid the groundwork and provided for leaders of Franciscan women's religious institutes the intellectual appreciation that solidified the ground beneath our feet.

The Ground on Which We Stand

The ground on which we stand can be described in terms of a number of organizations, movements, and structures that have played a role in Franciscan education since the early decades of the twentieth century.

The Sister Formation Movement

The Sister Formation Conference (SFC) was established in 1953 with the clear aim of improving the academic preparation of women religious in this country.[13] Ford Foundation funding created the Everett Conference in 1956 at which sisters with PhDs created an undergraduate curriculum for the many cooperating colleges and universities. With the leadership of the SFC many communities promoted studies for master's and doctoral degrees to insure adequate staffing for their own institutions. Summer Institutes convened major superiors and directors of formation, thus providing the first systematic training of formation personnel.[14] The Sister Formation Bulletin had enormous circulation since 85% of the superiors participating in the movement promoted its perusal in local houses. As organizations with related goals and intersecting purposes also worked on issues of modernizing the life and the

---

[13]Marjorie Noterman Beane, PhD, *From Framework to Freedom: A History of the Sister Formation Conference* (Lanham, MD: University Press of America, Inc., 1993).
[14]Lora Ann Quinonez, CDP, and Mary Daniel Turner, SNDdN, *The Transformation of American Catholic Sisters* (Philadelphia: Temple University Press, 1992), 8.

apostolates of U.S. women religious, tensions and triumphs abounded.

The work of the SFC was a response to new questions within congregations themselves and to the call of Pius XII for the modernization of the theological and professional education of young religious women. This call had been anticipated in the research of Sister Bertrande Meyers, DC, published in 1941. It found a ready hearing among many superiors of American congregations. Initial momentum came through the National Catholic Education Association (NCEA) where the desperate need for better preparation for service in the classroom was being admitted— though not without controversy. Between 1948 and 1954 many presentations and inquiries prepared the way for a bold initiative on behalf of religious women in their formative years. At the 1954 meeting of the NCEA, a separate Sisters Formation Conference was launched. Sister Emil Penet, IHM, who had already established herself as a fearless advocate of change, was charged with leadership of the group.

While the volume of material describing the SFC's work is substantial, suffice it to say that great stress was given to providing sisters with a bachelor's degree before sending them into their professional assignments. A juniorate program was proposed to extend the period of initial formation. This program emphasized the integration of intellectual development and the continued growth in religious discipline and spiritual maturity. Experimental curricula were introduced in colleges sponsored by congregations of sisters; and a new, wholistic approach to religious, professional, and human growth gradually became the norm. [15]

By the time of its dissolution in the 1960s, the SFC had made the U.S. sisters the most highly educated group of nuns in the Church, on a par with the most highly educated women in the country. It provided an inter-congregational platform for change. It created a paradigm that shaped a new self-determination among U.S. women religious. The legitimacy of aspiring to full academic excellence among Catholic women became a national priority. It paved the way for revolutionary changes in religious life. Its legacy is

---

[15]Among Franciscan religious participating in this work, the special leadership of Sister Emmanuel Collins of the Rochester, Minnesota, Franciscans and the role of St. Teresa's College in Winona must be given honorable mention.

now a matter of historical record, and thousands of women, lay and religious, are its beneficiaries.

The Franciscan Education Conference

In 1914 a meeting of rectors of Seraphic Colleges took place near Cleveland.[16] By 1919 a full fledged Franciscan Education Conference (FEC) was formed under the authority of the Provincials of the Order of Friars Minor. Plans called for a meeting connected to the annual Catholic Education Association Meeting, and the entire course of studies offered in the various provinces was up for consideration. Those targeted for invitations included prefects of studies, rectors and vice-rectors of preparatory seminaries, lectors in philosophy, and any others delegated by the superiors. By 1922 the Conventual and Capuchin branches were added. After twenty-five years the Third Order Regular friars and other brotherhoods of the Third Order Regular were included. The earliest motives for the founding of the conference were found in the friars' desire to improve the curriculum that prepared their young men for ordination and/or professional apostolic ministry. The conference drew upon the talent and vision of men from every part of the Franciscan family and benefited generations of young men who entered the Order's ranks. It also responded to the challenge of the charism that calls us to brotherhood *and* sisterhood.

The first notice of sisters being included in the FEC proceedings came in 1948. For the next three years, sisters were invited as guests to the annual meetings. Gradually the wisdom of developing a separate program prevailed. In 1952 four hundred sisters from thirty-five congregations attended the first National Conference of Franciscan Sisterhoods at the College of St. Francis in Joliet, Illinois. At first, the same friars who presented papers at the FEC later presented the same material to the sisters. When planning took place for the second national meeting, however, the

---

[16]The archives of the FEC are housed at St. Bonaventure University. In 1987, Sister Benedicta Dega, FSSJ, organized these files for future use. Mrs. Lorraine Welsh, present University archivist, has been most generous in assisting me. The material in this section is based on a review of these files. A more comprehensive study could be made with profit.

friar advisors advocated the promotion of sisters as presenters. Goals that appear in the minutes of these proceedings highlight the study of Franciscanism and the application of that study to teaching, nursing, and other apostolates.

The newly completed Alverno College in Milwaukee hosted the second event in 1953 and one thousand sisters attended. One of the noteworthy resolutions of this session was the request that the works of St. Bonaventure, the Seraphic Doctor, be made available in English as soon as possible. To read the archives of this organization and its male counterpart is to be alternately thrilled and humbled by the scope of what was done and what was dreamed of in those days before the birth of the Sister Formation Conference, by the availability of academic offerings on Franciscan sources,[17] and even by Paul VI's call in the Council's wake to recover the charism.

Imagine, if you can, the atmosphere of the meeting at which Thomas E. Murray, Chairman of the Atomic Energy Commission, gave an address called "The Problems of the Atomic Age," and Allan B. Wolter, OFM, presented the paper of the recently deceased Philotheus Boehner, OFM, called "The Teaching of the Sciences." This session called participants to appreciation of the work of scientists, the understanding of the physical and biological world, and the acquisition of objective methods of inquiry. Its theme was "Nature, the Mirror of God."

We take heart from these examples of early collaboration between sisters and brothers of the family. However the skies were not cloudless. Undoubtedly, the models of work and study being generated with the Sister Formation Movement began to influence the situation. Inevitable tensions led to more autonomy for the sisters' organization. By 1960 it existed as the Franciscan Sisters Education Conference (FSEC) and annual dues ($25) were being requested from major superiors. In 1962 at the eleventh meeting, held at Marian College in Indianapolis, plans were being made for a complete separation that would provide a" sisters only" executive

---

[17]A single example of the kind of ambitions this environment created might be the master's dissertation by Irene Deger, OSF, of the School Sisters of Milwaukee. As a student at Regina Mundi, she completed in 1957 a remarkable study entitled "The Impact of the Franciscan Ideal of Poverty on Society in the Thirteenth Century." At a time when few Franciscan women had the training to contextualize this theme, she succeeded. Her fine work was not published for the larger Franciscan family. Some of the factors described below may well acount for this.

board and planning committee. The new constitution and by-laws of the organization offered the following explanation of goals:

> This organization purposes to bear witness to the living spirit of St. Francis by bringing to bear his mind, which is the mind of the VIR CATHOLICUS, upon the problems of the times and upon the particular and contemporary needs of the Franciscan Sisterhoods. This will be accomplished primarily through the annual Franciscan Sisters' Educational Conference which will provide these Sisterhoods with the opportunity of mutual sharing of knowledge and experience.

It is important to note that part of the evolution of the organization was towards inclusion of congregations that were not primarily engaged in teaching. Gradually, the desire to promote apostolic effectiveness was being matched by interest in studying Franciscan religious life itself. Thus we find the twelfth conference moving to the topic of formation. It is also important to stress the fact that whatever difficulties may have been experienced in creating a separate sisters conference, continuing support and interest on the part of the friars is evident in more than one archival communication. The date 1969 is on the last document describing a national sisters meeting under the auspices of the FSEC.

The Franciscan Federation

In 1965 the first meeting of major superiors destined to found the Franciscan Federation of the U.S.A. took place. Within a few years the Franciscan Sisters Education Conference ceased to function, as the Federation grew into the dominant form of participation in renewal among communities of Franciscan women. The earliest efforts of the Federation met with enthusiasm. Thus, many sisters may not have realized that its very success was threatening the existence of the FSEC. It is entirely possible that many Franciscan sisters simply assumed that the Federation was a natural successor to FSEC. For others, a lingering regret continued to surface for some years, thus indicating a painful denouement of this valiant organization. With the advantage of hindsight we can now see that the Federation did, indeed, meet the new and urgent needs of dealing with questions of identity and formation at all levels. What it could not absorb with equal energy was a commitment to serving, as the FSEC had done, as a resource for educators per se. If today we ask about the role and influence of women in an academic realm of Franciscan scholarship, it may be that we are unwittingly resurrecting the heritage of the FSEC.

In any event, it is a welcome chance we have at this juncture to remember and acclaim the monumental efforts that were spent in pursuit of educational excellence by the Franciscan women of an earlier American epoch.[18]

The Franciscan Institute

The first doctorate awarded by the Franciscan Institute was to Sister Emma Therese Healy, CSJ, of Erie, Pennsylvania.[19] Her thesis was "St. Bonaventure's *Reductio Artium ad Theologiam*." The year was 1939.[20] Events that led to the Institute's beginnings go back to 1930 and the efforts of Thomas Plassmann, OFM, then president of St. Bonaventure University. However, it was the arrival of Philotheus Boehner, OFM—also in 1939—that was to give new purpose and cohesion to this study center in western New York state. Boehner identified Franciscan studies as history, missiology, spirituality, and philosophy. The odyssey of the Institute in its relationship to the general curia of the Friars Minor, to the provinces of the United States, in particular Holy Name Province, and to the university's governing bodies is a "long and winding road." Throughout that history, women, especially Franciscan sisters, have been part of the journey. Some came as students, benefiting from the opportunity to gain both a Master's degree in any of the four fields and a Doctoral degree in philosophy. Others

---

[18]Elise Saggau, OSF, details the role played by the Federation in her paper, included in this publication, pp. 105-11.

[19]Conrad L. Harkins, "General History of the Franciscan Institute," *Franciscan Studies*, 51 (1991): 7-68.

[20]This was also the year that Catholic University published the doctoral thesis of Mary Rachel Dady, OSF, on "The Theory of Knowledge of St. Bonaventure," which was to be the first volume of the University's philosophy series. Mary Rachel was a Rochester, Minnesota, Franciscan.

came as staff members, giving long-term assistance with publications. Notable in the archives are Sisters Frances Laughlin SMIC, Emma Jane Spargo, SNJM, and Mary Anthony Brown, OSF.

The teaching program was suspended in 1961. In 1972, under the direction of Conrad Harkins, OFM, the Institute once again welcomed students, this time offering a new curriculum of Franciscan studies leading to a Master of Arts degree. The simple fact that the Institute's program allowed women to attain academic credibility in a field so thoroughly dominated by men for centuries can hardly be overestimated in its importance. The Institute student body has included hundreds of women, over the years, lay and religious. Eleven women have served as faculty or staff members from the "second generation" school to the present.[21]

Joliet, Washington, Berkeley

Even though time does not permit a full description of the next three centers, it would be a serious omission not to offer some indication of their importance. The first no longer exists; the other two are vital contemporary centers of Franciscan education.

The Seraphic Institute of the College of St. Francis in Joliet, Illinois, operated from 1954 until 1970. The purpose of the program was to present "in a scientific way, the contributions of illustrious Franciscan scholars who flourished from the thirteenth century until the present day." The program offered a certificate or a master of arts degree. The friars of Assumption Province were the backbone of the faculty for the Institute. The curriculum planning was meticulous as was the administrative oversight of the Sisters of St. Francis of Mary Immaculate. The concerns of the SFC are mirrored in the archival documents.[22] Sisters whose own Franciscan vocations would be strengthened by exposure to these courses had a three-summer program available in addition to other theological offerings. Graduate degrees could be earned by those committed to the "use of original sources and seminar work." By the time of its

---

[21]The issue of *Franciscan Studies* cited above also contains a register of students and faculty that provides additional data. See 153-219.

[22]Materials taken from the archives of The Sisters of St. Francis in Joliet, Illinois. My thanks to archivist, Marian Voelker, OSF, for her generous cooperation.

termination the Seraphic Institute had awarded seventy master's degrees and two hundred and sixty-one certificates.

The Franciscan School of Theology opened in Berkeley in 1968. The friars of the Saint Barbara Province embraced a new context for theological education and a new constituency for their programs. The friars for whom this school was the ground of theological preparation were coming from a rather "cloistered" existence at Old Mission Santa Barbara to the ferment of Berkeley in the late 60s. From its inception this program included women. The decision to open the program was revolutionary and required considerable courage. In the thirty years since, it has been home to many women seeking a broad preparation for ministry within the Franciscan academic ambience. Numerous women have benefited from the expertise of Franciscan faculty members in developing a thesis or major paper. The sabbatical offerings draw numerous women from many countries.

The Franciscan Chair at Washington Theological Union was the gift of Holy Name and Immaculate Conception Provinces of the Friars Minor in 1989. The most recent addition to the possibilities for graduate Franciscan education, it provides a strong focus for Franciscan women in both sabbatical and degree programs. The symposia annually sponsored by the Chair offer many women the chance for scholarly exchange and publication of their work.

Nor should we fail to note that there are numerous faculties of theology in this country—and even a few of philosophy—where scholars with a Franciscan focus have encouraged women to adopt thesis projects or intellectual options that benefit the "gross national product" of Franciscan knowledge. One thinks of the impact of professors such as Ewert Cousins, Zachary Hayes, OFM, Margaret Guider, OSF, Mary Beth Ingham, CSJ, and Marilyn McCord Adams—to offer a few good examples.

Conclusion

This brings us to the conclusion of considerations founded on two important points:

1) Franciscan studies must be defined broadly—as indeed it is by its best practitioners—so that we do not develop a

myopic sense of whose contributions "count." While recognizing the matrix of areas that were first spelled out years ago, we need to attend to a variety of fields to appreciate the contributions of all women to our work.

2) Women are making a contribution to Franciscan studies today that is visible in new ways in new places. However, careful examination of the organizations and movements that preceded Vatican II shows the presence of a long and honored line of women who did much to seed the ground from which we have harvested renewed possibilities. We should take care to retell their stories and to join them to our own.

While I have not developed the following considerations, I consider them worth listing for further development in our conversation:

1) To this point in time the academic possibilities for women have been located in Western/Northern countries. In Asia, Latin America, and Africa there has been strong service in Franciscan renewal and theology. However, the pursuit of academic foundations by women in these areas has not always been possible. As more women from Southern/Eastern cultures deal with their questions and our tradition, we will need to be very attentive to the impact of such exploration upon many of our assumptions and patterns of interpretation.

2) The amount of work that needs to be done to initiate, coordinate, and refine studies of Franciscan women and their contributions through history is staggering. We need to acknowledge how "early" in this movement we stand and be ready for a long, long journey.

3) Getting academic credentials does not always translate into getting adequate employment with those credentials. Women cannot be encouraged to enter or remain in this field if, once a degree is earned, the subject of one's work must be relegated to the background while

the hard facts of earning a living dominate one's possibilities.

4) Women have to decide how much they are willing to sacrifice in order to gain and maintain a visible presence and a palpable impact in this field. It is also very important for us to be aware of the major shifts that have occurred among religious women in regard to the intellectual life. The Brookland Commission has given us substantial documentation on the loss of commitment to liberal education among women religious in the past thirty years. Thus, one of the significant pools of potential scholarship has long been moving away from this kind of commitment. Encouraging *that* cohort of women to take up the challenge is particularly daunting.

We may need, therefore, to look at the historical record to determine what factors favored intellectual commitment in the past and what factors in the present favor a return to higher studies for specializations as specific as the one we are discussing. We will need a way to overcome the duality present in this paper—the constant need to juxtapose information pertaining to women religious with the recognition that increasing numbers of laywomen are doing work in this area. Is there, after all, any corporate or communal effort that can be promoted to insure a better future for women's Franciscan scholarship?

The surveys I have done of the organizations described above are replete with reminders about the hard work, the creative commitment, the energetic determination needed for such undertakings. Are we ready for a new task of this magnitude?

APPENDIX

The following is a reproduction/translation of the General Index of the *Bibliographia Franciscana* published in *Collectanea Franciscana* by the Capuchin Historical Insititute in Rome since 1929. (This particular index is from Volume 18, 1993-1994.) I have retained the Latin titles for each division, but have provided an English version of subdivisions. It should be noted that many of the subdivisions listed here are further separated into more precise categories. For example, the section on national histories of the First Order includes eighteen national subdivisions.

I. *Subsidia et Instrumenta*
   1. Historiography
   2. Bibliography and encyclopediae
   3. Catalogs of mss., editions, sources

II. *S. Franciscus Assisiensis*
   1. Franciscan sources: Writings of S. Francis
   2. Franciscan sources: The "old" *legendae*
   3. Modern biography
   4. Biographical studies
   4. Spirituality
   5. Apostolic action
   6. Cult and devotion
   7. Arts, letters, music

III. *Studia et Doctrinae*
   1. Studies
   2. Philosophy and theology
   3. Spirituality
   4. Liturgy
   5. Renovation and religious institutes
   6. Apostolates
   7. Particular Law

IV. *Scriptores*
1. Writers of the 13th Century
2. Writers of the 14th Century
3. Writers of the 15th Century
     . . . and so on until the 20th Century

V. *Primus Ordo Franciscanus*
1. Universal history
2. National history

VI. *Missiones*
1. General
2. Geographic distribution

VII. *S. Clara et Secundus Ordo*
1. S. Clare of Assisi
2. Second Order

VIII. *Tertius Ordo Regularis*
1. Masculine congregations
2. Feminine congregations

IX. *Ordo Franciscanus Saecularis et Sodalica*
1. Secular Franciscan Order: General
2. Secular Franciscan Order by nation
3. Cordeliers, sodalities, secular institutes

X. *Ars, Litterae, Musica*
1. Arts
2. Literature
3. Music

It is clear that experts in a vast array of specializations can and do make contributions to Franciscan studies as judged by this important "arbiter" of Franciscan scholarship, the *Bibliographia Franciscana*.

The Franciscan Federation as a Promoter of Women's Scholarship
Response to Margaret Carney

Elise Saggau, OSF

Background

The Franciscan Federation of the Brothers and Sisters of the Third Order Regular had its roots in movements taking place among United States religious even before Vatican Council II.[1] The Sister Formation Conference in the fifties and sixties was especially effective in raising the consciousness of religious women, impelling them to look for greater opportunities to improve their own professional preparedness and theological background.

Concomitant with the sister formation movement among American women religious was the development of the Franciscan Sisters' Educational Conference (FSEC), an off-shoot of the Franciscan Educational Conference (FEC) begun by the Friars Minor as early as 1919.[2] The FSEC had a separate existence in the American Franciscan family from 1952 until 1976. Though its purpose was often misunderstood as being a service to teaching sisters, its express purpose was

> to study and to bear witness to the living, developing spirit of Saint Francis as it encounters the challenges of our times and the contemporary needs of Franciscan Sisters. The purpose is accomplished primarily through the annual Franciscan Sisters Conference which will provide these Sisters with the opportunity of mutual sharing of knowledge and experience.[3]

---

[1]For a more detailed history of the Federation, cf. Elise Saggau, OSF, *A Short History of The Franciscan Federation* (Washington, DC: The Franciscan Federation, 1995).

[2]Cf. Pius J. Barth, OFM, "The Franciscan View of Education," *Franciscan Education*, Report of the First National Meeting of Franciscan Teaching Sisterhoods, Joliet, IL, College of St. Francis, Nov. 28-29, 1952, p. 7.

[3]From the Constitutions of the FSEC as quoted by Sister Mary Grace Peters in a one-page undated document, "Continuation of the History of the Franciscan Sisters Conference," in files of the Franciscan Federation Office, Washington, DC.

By 1975, however, the ten-year-old Federation of Franciscan Sisters was beginning to meet many of the needs which the FSEC had been targeting. This fact, as well as other logistic and financial problems, put the continued existence of the FSEC into question, and, on January 24, 1976, the organization came to an end.[4]

The Franciscan Federation

The new Federation, when it was founded in 1965, explicitly recognized its role in promoting the intellectual gifts of Franciscan women and the need to foster cooperative efforts between Franciscan women and men. It decided to pursue the following goals (among others):

- to produce a "spiritual document"
- to establish "rededication" programs at St. Bonaventure, NY
- to encourage attendance at the Seraphic Institute, St. Francis College, Joliet, Illinois
- to establish a speakers' bureau composed of competent Franciscan men and women religious who would travel to Franciscan communities
- to establish a research committee and a continuing education committee
- to establish relationships with Franciscan publishing houses

In 1970 the executive board of the Federation and the board which coordinated workshops on the new spiritual document met with the English-speaking Conference of the Order of Friars Minor in Wappinger Falls, New York, to share insights on Franciscan life and prayer. Father David Eckelkamp, OFM, secretary of the Conference, expressed his appreciation and hope that this was the beginning of communication among men and women major superiors of Franciscan congregations. He looked forward to seeing "what great things can be accomplished when great numbers of Brothers and Sisters work together in unity and harmony for the building up of God's Kingdom!"[5]

---

[4]Peters.
[5]Memo to the Federation boards, May 8, 1970; from the Federation files.

Creation of Spiritual Documents

Active, apostolic congregations of Franciscan women in the United States, in trying to renew themselves, did not find the Third Order Rule of 1927 very helpful. Thus the Federation undertook to produce a document that would supply underlying values and directions for the renewal of their congregations. A committee made up of seven volunteers from six different member congregations developed the new spiritual document, following these principles:

- It must be true to the Franciscan charism and be able to inspire and motivate contemporary Franciscan religious women.
- It must draw from the whole body of Francis's own writings.
- It must be based on Gospel principles and on Francis's own special insights and applicable to religious life and mission in our times.
- It would include five fundamental principles: Littleness (Minority), Fraternity, Obedience, Prayer (Contemplation), and Fulfillment in Personal Freedom. Its point of departure was Francis's conversion experience.[6]

The document was entitled *Go to My Brethren*, inspired by the Gospel missionary mandate which sent the women away from the empty tomb to bring the good news of the Resurrection to the disciples and to the world.

The development of *Go to My Brethren* was concomitant with similar projects going on in Europe, notably in France, Belgium, Luxembourg, and Holland. It also corresponded to a similar effort by the fourth Franciscan Tertiary Inter-Obediential Congress in Madrid, Spain, which produced in 1974 "A Statement of Understanding of Franciscan Penitential Life," also called the Madrid Statement. Sister Rose Margaret Delaney, SFP, who was

---

[6]Anne Carville, OSF, "History," p. 17. (This is a short history of the Federation presented at the twenty-fifth anniversary gathering in Pittsburgh in August, 1990. It can be found in the files of the Franciscan Federation, Washington, DC.)

then the President of the Franciscan Federation, represented the Federation at this Congress.

A New Rule

But it was only in October, 1979, that an international meeting of general superiors of Third Order Regular women was convened in Assisi for the express purpose of considering a new Rule of life for Franciscan women. Sister Roberta Cusack, OSF, as Executive Director of the U.S. Federation, was sent to this meeting as the Federation's official representative. The group looked at three texts as possible foundations for a new Rule—the Madrid Statement, the Holland Rule, and the French Rule for Franciscan Sisters.

While undertaking work on a new Rule, the group was also developing a structure for an on-going international organization. It soon became clear that this International Franciscan Conference (CFI) would have to include the Third Order Regular men's congregations, a step which was immediately implemented. An international commission including men and women members was set up to work on the Rule text, to which Roberta Cusack was appointed early in 1980. Later that spring Margaret Carney, OSF, was also appointed to the commission. In August, 1980, she wrote:

> Members of the Third Order Regular are confidently, gladly, responding to the promptings of the Spirit that urge them to "make all things new." Perhaps the most important aspect of this period of tertiary history is not the possibility of a new version of the Rule in this century, but the possibility of a renewed allegiance to the vital tradition of the Third Order Regular of St. Francis. This new allegiance and élan is already experienced in many religious congregations and is itself worth the struggle to discern the true imprint of Francis in the documents that shape our lives.[7]

In 1981 Margaret Carney and Thaddeus Hogan, SA, were the American representatives on the International Work Group which

---

[7]Margaret Carney, OSF, *Federation Newsletter* (August, 1980): 17.

was developing the new Rule. The goal was to have a proposed text ready for the meeting of the International Conference in March, 1982, in Rome. This meeting was attended by approximately two hundred general superiors, the vast majority of whom were women. They represented thirty-five countries and 200,000 Third Order Regular religious women and men world-wide. This group approved the new Rule text with some modifications and, on December 8, 1982, it was officially approved by Pope John Paul II in a papal brief, *Franciscanum Vita Propositum.*

The Federation, under the executive directorship of Anne Carville, OSF, was very active in disseminating information about the new Rule among American Third Order Regular religious and about the theology and tradition behind it. Many workshops, called "Roots and Wings," were held around the country, and a series of substantial theological reflections, called *Propositi*, were published in the Federation newsletter.

Other Federation Undertakings

In 1981 the Franciscan Federation formally reconstituted itself to include Third Order Regular men's congregations. Working together on the international Rule project had made clear the necessity of the brothers and sisters collaborating in many other aspects of their Franciscan Third Order life.

From 1982 to 1989 the Federation also was active in promoting the work of the Third Order Regular scholar, Raffaele Pazzelli. His book on the history of the Franciscan penitential movement had been published in Italy in 1982. It promoted new insights into the nature and history of the penitential way of life. With the help and support of the Federation, an English translation was published in the United States in 1989. [8]

In 1986, the Federation, in collaboration with Margaret Pirkl, OSF, published *Monographs on a Global Perspective*, articles written by Franciscans from all over the world.

In 1990, on the twenty-fifth anniversary of the Federation, the membership undertook a much needed re-organization. The newly-

---

[8]Raffaele Pazzelli, TOR, *St. Francis and the Third Order: The Franciscan and Pre-Franciscan Penitential Movement* (Chicago: Franciscan Herald Press, 1989).

formulated goals specifically included "continued support for Franciscan scholarship and education." This aspect of the Federation's self-understanding had never waned over the years.

Under the executive directorship of Sister Kathleen Moffatt, OSF, (1991-1995), the Federation supported only one standing committee—the Spirit and Life Committee—which assumed responsibility for carrying out the study goals of the organization. In 1992 this committee prepared articles for the September issue of *The Cord* magazine as part of the celebration of the tenth anniversary of the 1982 Rule. In 1993 the committee collaborated on the workshop, "Build with Living Stones/TOR," at Mission San Luis Rey, California, and also formed part of the steering committee for a symposium at Neumann College in Aston, Pennsylvania, on the Franciscan charism and college faculty development. The Spirit and Life Committee continues to be a creative and energizing force behind the educational programs of the Federation.

In August, 1992, the Federation collaborated with other Franciscans in offering a networking symposium in Denver, Colorado, on "The Franciscan Experience of Christ in North America," and in June, 1993, it supported the efforts of Midwest Franciscans in Collaboration in hosting "Clarefest 93: Word and Image" at Viterbo College in LaCrosse, Wisconsin. This celebration of the eight-hundredth anniversary of Clare's birth gathered a significant number of women, as well as men, scholars to explore the meaning of Clare for us today. In the same year the Federation published *Clare Study Guidelines*, prepared by Helen Budzik, OSF.

In July, 1994, at St. Bonaventure University, the Federation offered a historic seminar on the 1982 Rule, revisiting the unique collaborative international experience that had produced the "new" Rule and exploring its contemporary applications and the distinct nature of the penitential tradition. Kathleen Moffatt followed up this event by preparing *Resources for the Study of the Third Order Regular Rule*, an impressive collection of articles and materials both historical and reflective, which the Federation published.

In January, 1995, the Federation co-sponsored, with the Franciscan School of Theology, Berkeley, a symposium on

Franciscan Christology, the presentations of which were later published in *The Cord* (May/June, 1995). The increasing interest in Franciscan Christology gave birth to a workshop, "Facing the Christ Incarnate," which the Federation sponsored in many places across the country. This multi-faceted program teamed up brothers and sisters of the different branches of the Franciscan Family. As a follow-up to these workshops, Kathleen Moffatt prepared a comprehensive *Resource Manual for the Study of Franciscan Christology*, published by the Federation in 1998.

The Franciscan Federation has supported and encouraged educational and research projects and programs that have given women increasing opportunities to use their gifts both in the service of the Third Order Regular branch of the Family, as well as in service to the greater Franciscan Order. Women scholars have found opportunities through Federation-sponsored programs, both national and local, to share their gifts, to further the Franciscan intellectual tradition, and to create a new image of women in scholarly roles in the Order.

The Cord has certainly profited by the programs of the Franciscan Federation and has in its turn been able to provide publication opportunities for women scholars and other women who have made a serious commitment to Franciscan study.

What Difference Does It Make?

What difference does it make that women's voices are being heard more clearly and more respectfully in the Franciscan Family? What difference does it make that we are engaging in experiences of mutuality in the academic community? There is no scientific answer to this question yet, but if we stand side by side with the men of the Order, it seems reasonable to suppose that we will feel more responsibility for the kind of Order it is. We will feel more confident that the experiences of women count in the future shaping of this "Family." Our hope is that this greater mutuality will help form a community of brothers and sisters that more effectively reflects the way of life envisioned by Jesus Christ for the human family and that Francis envisioned when he declared that our Rule, our *forma vitae*, is the Gospel.

A Personal Experience
Response to Margaret Carney

Roberta A. Mc Kelvie, OSF

I am here today as the latest recipient of the benefits of the trajectory begun with the Franciscan Educational Conference. On the list of the participants from 1960, which Margaret Carney has shared with us, the first four names are those of the Superior General and three Provincials of the Bernardine Sisters. I am very much aware that I continue a process begun long ago.

In order to give my response, it will be helpful if you allow me to include a partial telling of my own story, how I happen to be sitting here before you today. I do this not because it happened to me, but because it illustrates the kinds of things we have been discussing in this symposium. I did not intend to become a research scholar when I began my studies at the Franciscan Institute. At the time, my interest was in the area of spirituality and praxis. I never dreamed what the outcome would be. In the years I studied at the Institute, there were always the questions: "Where are the women? Where are the stories about the Franciscan women?" We had a significantly large group of Third Order women there, and we all asked the same questions. It was only in my second or third summer there that Regis Armstrong, OFM Cap., taught a course with a focus on Clare.

It is important for you to know that I did not start out as a feminist. It happened along the way, because, given the resources I had, it was the right way to go. This brings me to my first point: women in Franciscan studies face a major issue almost immediately. You will recall Gabriele Uhlein's comment that radical feminism rejects all aspects of patriarchal tradition as irredeemable, but some forms of feminism claim that there are things which can and should be preserved. We Third Order women have all been trained with an absolute awareness that the charism has always included the commitment of obedience to the Church and to the Holy Father. This was always in front of us as we studied the Rule. Today, Franciscan studies and feminism highlight the difficulties of fidelity to this tradition in light of patriarchal practices, especially in light of fidelity to one's personal vocation or congregational charism.

My own difficulties with the pervasiveness of patriarchy began when, as an assignment in Maurice Sheehan's (OFM,Cap.) class, I read Omer Englebert's biography of Francis. In his chapter on Clare he says: "A woman is generally worth what the ideas of the man she admires are worth, and her capacity for sacrifice allows her to attain the heights of heroism when the man shows her the way. Thus it was for St. Clare. . . ." The first time I read this I was besieged with disbelief. This was not the Clare I wanted to be connected to![1]

During my first summer at the Institute, I had taken the course on the Sources and on the History of the Order. I was the only woman in the group; the other thirty-two students were friars, novices, scholastics, and so on. It was an interesting experience for me. In a six-week program, we spent five weeks on the First Order, maybe two days on the Second Order, and one day on the Third Order. That was the picture of the Franciscan world as a whole that most friars knew.

Eventually I went to Fordham and encountered Elizabeth Johnson and Maryanne Kowaleski, forceful feminists both. At one point I submitted a paper to Maryanne, a revision and expansion of work I had done for Regis Armstrong at the Institute. It came back awash in red ink, more red ink than I had seen in twenty years of education! I asked myself, what am I missing here? In reading the comments, I became aware of problems with language (e.g., "fraternity" with its male connotations), with questions of male dominance and oppressive praxis, and I began to re-evaluate the way I had learned the stories of Franciscan life.

As far as theology was concerned, my response for the first six months I was at Fordham was: "What does this have to do with my life?" I had had the same difficulty when I began at the Institute, because so much of the material seemed to me to be founded upon abstract thought and ultra-scholastic considerations. But the reason I went on to doctoral studies was to have my work on Angelina of Montegiove given appropriate recognition, and I had finally

---

[1]Omer Englebert, *Saint Francis of Assisi: A Biography*, trans. Eve Marie Cooper (Chicago: Franciscan Herald Press, 1966), 160.

admitted that the magic letters "Ph.D." were necessary to have any chance for that to happen. So I assiduously did the course work, took what I could from the material that was put before me, and did what I had to do. By the time I reached the stage of working on my dissertation, Ewert Cousins, Elizabeth Johnson, and Richard Gyug in the history department shepherded me through the process of research, and my project on Angelina came to fruition.

None of this would have happened without the collaborative effort and support of the friars at the Institute who first encouraged me to go on in my studies—even when I laughed and said it was the farthest thing from my mind. Michael Blastic, OFM, Romuald Green, OFM, Regis Armstrong, and others—all opened doors by way of their encouragement long before I was ready to admit the need for doctoral studies. So the collaboration that Elise referred to has been an essential part of my educational story and my life as a Franciscan woman.

The Angelina project began as an independent study paper for Regis Armstrong after Margaret Carney had said to me one summer: "You (!) should do Angelina," because she had met one of my Sisters who had told her about a stained glass window we have in our chapel in Reading which is a representation of Angelina. At the end of the summer, I went to Reading and looked at the window and said to myself: "What are you doing here?" And the chase was on. I was willing to undertake it because what I had read about the Beguines resonated with my own community experience. There was something there I could not name. Also, there was my reaction when Dominic Monti, in trying to explain the word "Beguine" in his history class, downplayed the linguistic history of the Italian word. I had spent most of my life to that time teaching English, and I was really unhappy with the way he just brushed aside the evolution of language. So my search for Angelina's story was motivated by both personal and scholarly interest.

Finally, some specific references to the rest of the symposium.

1) We discussed the language question, especially the word "fraternity." There was a time I did not like the word or use it freely, but that changed as I came to understand its roots in Francis's thought. It comes from the theological understanding that Jesus is our brother, the first of our brothers and sisters, and that we

are all sisters and brothers by way of *his* brotherhood. Once we begin to look at the word with that fundamental idea, we can change our perspective on "fraternity" as exclusively male or hierarchical. We can see ourselves as sister or brother to all of creation and to each other. That makes an amazing difference.

2) There has been some emphasis on texts written by Francis, Clare, Angela of Foligno, etc. What happens, as in my case, when there are no texts? We have no words of Angelina, and if there ever were any, they were destroyed during the time of the French Revolution, if not before. So, did that make her an unfit subject for study? No. It meant only that another way had to be found. This is one of the things women in Franciscan studies are doing—finding new ways to deal with old material, old stories, and incomplete information.

3) When the resources of texts are missing, the work can be done only if the brothers and sisters collaborate. The friars have libraries that we do not; they have the ability and the generosity to share them with us. I know that if Michael Higgins, TOR, had not provided access to the library at Ss. Cosmas and Damian in Rome, I might still be looking for my first copy of a biography of Angelina. There were people like Nancy Celaschi, OSF, at the International Franciscan Conference, who does yeoman's work as a clearing house and contact person. There were also the Felician Sisters at their Generalate in Rome who housed me during my second trip for research. All of the women in Franciscan studies need not be scholars!

4) When it comes to the feminist critique, each person has to decide where to stand. For me, there are many things that are worthwhile and valuable in Franciscan studies. I received some criticism because my critique was "not strong enough." I chose to omit some material which exemplified hierarchical oppression and I chose not to do "friar bashing" at every opportunity. There is a question of loyalty, of gratitude for support, of recognition of the good as well as the not-so-good. Responsible critique in Franciscan studies is important, but we ought not lose sight of the fact that our connections are not optional.

Bonaventure's Trinitarian Theology as a Feminist Resource

Maria Calisi, PhD

Introduction

My work in Franciscan theology deals primarily with using Bonaventure as a resource for feminist Trinitarian theology. I am immeasurably and profoundly indebted to the scholarly work of the late Professor Catherine Mowry LaCugna for giving me a direction in which to take Bonaventurian theology. Two of her works have been particularly helpful: her book, *God For Us: The Trinity and Christian Life* and her chapter on the Trinity in a work she edited, entitled *Freeing Theology: The Essentials of Theology in Feminist Perspective*.[1] I have come to share her concern that the doctrine of the Trinity has become divorced from Catholic life and practice. I also share LaCugna's position that

> [t]he doctrine of the Trinity is ultimately a practical doctrine with radical consequences for Christian life. . . . The doctrine of the Trinity is ultimately therefore a teaching not about the abstract nature of God, nor about God in isolation from everything other than God, but a teaching about God's life with us and our life with each other. Trinitarian theology could be described as a theology of relationship par excellence, which explores the mysteries of love, relationship, personhood, and communion within the framework of God's self-revelation in the person of Christ and the activity of the Spirit."[2]

LaCugna's works resonate with Bonaventure's works, and we have in Bonaventure a Trinitarian model which is well-suited to her goal of restoring the doctrine of the Trinity as the central doctrine of salvation, as "the proper source for reflection on theological

---

[1] Catherine Mowry LaCugna, *God For Us: The Trinity and Christian Life* (San Francisco: HarperCollins, 1991), 1.
   Catherine Mowry LaCugna, "God in Communion With Us: The Trinity," in *Freeing Theology: The Essentials of Theology in Feminist Perspective*, ed. Catherine Mowry LaCugna (San Francisco: HarperCollins, 1993), 83-114.
[2] *God For Us*, 1.

ethics, spirituality, ecclesiology, and the liturgical and communitarian life of the Church."[3]

The Next Generation: the Potential of Franciscan Studies to Address Modern Theological Questions

The next generation in Franciscan studies, that is the future of Franciscan studies, lies, in part, in its ability to address important theological and social issues from a solid foundation in the Christian tradition. Theological inquiry should maintain a tension between "continuity and development" in the tradition. This tension is necessary to preserve the integrity of revealed truth while addressing genuinely new and profoundly essential questions about power and justice, about women's roles, and even about the nature of women's humanity.

The Franciscan tradition is well suited to maintaining this balance of "continuity and development" in doing theology. In particular, the Franciscan tradition, *as interpreted and synthesized by Bonaventure*, has much to contribute to the dialogue that women have begun.

Before arriving at the main thesis of this paper, I present three examples in order to demonstrate the various ways that this untapped tradition can be mined as a theological resource.

The first example is Bonaventure's doctrine that the soul is a Trinitarian image. His theological anthropology, that is, his view of human nature, is wholesome, uplifting, and positive. It speaks of human dignity, in that the human soul is created as an image of the Trinity and every person reflects the triune God—Father, Son, and Spirit—in the human faculties of memory, intellect, and free will. Because we all bear the divine image within our souls, we have a natural, innate openness to God and a supernatural end or purpose. Bonaventure says we even have a innate knowledge of God. His doctrine of the soul as a Trinitarian image offers us a deeply rooted tradition from which to construct a theological anthropology based on human dignity and on a single, common human nature shared by men and women.

---

[3]*God For Us*, 1.

A second example of a point of departure for theological anthropology is derived from Franciscan spirituality, i.e., the devotion to the humanity of Christ. Feminist Christians have legitimately posed the question, "Can a male savior save women?"[4] The doctrine of the Incarnation is concerned with the union of Christ's divinity and humanity, *not* with his maleness. From the very beginning, the Christian community defended Christ's full humanity as a matter of salvation, for it was governed by the axiom that "What is not assumed [by the Logos] is not redeemed, but what is assumed is saved by union with God." Also from the very beginning, it was unquestioned that women were fully included in the human nature assumed by Christ. However, Christ's maleness has sometimes been used to justify the superiority of men over women, the headship of the husband over the wife, and the belief that only men can "image Christ." This is precisely the reason offered for the exclusion of women from ordained ministry—that only male priests have the capacity to "image Christ."[5]

The authentic Franciscan devotion to the humanity of Christ never emphasized his maleness, but emphasized his humanity in solidarity with the whole suffering human race. It is a spirituality lived *by both men and women* as an imitation of Christ, especially imitating Christ's humility, poverty, and love.[6] Franciscan meditations on the life of Christ have traditionally focused on the quintessential events that frame human life—birth and death.

A third example of the potential for Franciscan studies in the next generation is concerned with ecology and our stewardship of

---

[4]Cf.: Rosemary Radford Ruether, *Sexism and God-talk: Toward a Feminist Theology* (Boston: Beacon Press, 1983), 116-38 and *To Change the World: Christology and Cultural Criticism* (New York: Crossroad, 1981), 45-56; Elizabeth A. Johnson, "Redeeming the Name of Christ," in *Freeing Theology: The Essentials of Theology in Feminist Perspective*, ed. Catherine Mowry LaCugna (San Francisco: HarperCollins, 1993), 115-137; Anne E. Carr, *Transforming Grace: Christian Tradition and Women's Experience* (San Francisco: HarperCollins, 1988), 158-79.

[5]Sacred Congregation for the Doctrine of the Faith, "Inter Insigniores," (Declaration on the Question of the Admission of Women to the Ministerial Priesthood) *Origins* 6:33 (Feb. 3, 1977), par. 27.

The fact that Bonaventure is, perhaps, the first to use precisely this argument to exclude women from ordination cannot be discussed here. His position that women cannot "naturally represent Christ" because they are not male is simply inconsistent with his anthropological theology in general. Cf. Bonaventure, *Commentarius in librum sententiarum IV*, d.25, a.2, q.1, concl.

[6]For a discussion on the imitation of Christ, see Zachary Hayes, *The Hidden Center: Spirituality and Speculative Christology in Bonaventure* (New York: Paulist Press, 1981), 25-52.

the earth, the new field of eco-theology. Bonaventure's doctrine of exemplarity[7] would be a foundation from which to build a Christian eco-theology. Exemplarity is a doctrine that states that all created things are exemplifications of the Trinity, that is, each creature bears an imprint or a trace of the Trinity. Francis experienced God, encountered God, in creation; Bonaventure gave theological articulation to Francis's experience in his doctrine of exemplarity. Somewhat like considering a work of art as an expression of the artist, Bonaventure saw in nature the expression of the Father, Son, and Spirit as divine power, wisdom, and goodness.[8] Bonaventure calls all created things in the universe Trinitarian vestiges because they reflect God's power, wisdom, and goodness; but human beings are more than vestiges. They are divine images because they reflect the Father, Son, and Spirit in their capacity for, and function of, memory, intellect, and will.[9]

The Franciscan tradition, and Bonaventurian theology in particular, is a treasure trove of spiritual insight, mystical experience, philosophical speculation, ageless wisdom, doctrinal integrity, and adherence to revealed truth. It is a solid foundation from which to address modern theological questions in the areas of theological anthropology, feminist theology, Trinitarian theology, eco-theology, and Christology. My work in this tradition has centered on the current theological debate or dialogue about the Trinitarian naming of God. Women are posing such questions as: Are the names Father, Son, and Spirit *proper* names or relational names? Do the male metaphors in theological discourse and in liturgy lead to the impression that God is male? Does the exclusive use of male names and metaphors for God harm women and perpetuate the oppression of women? If the answers to these three question are yes, should we change or augment the traditional Trinitarian formula? My research[10] offers three points of entry into this dialogue:

---

[7]Cf. Bonaventure, *The Soul's Journey into God*, chs. 1 and 2, trans. Ewert Cousins, The Classics of Western Spirituality (New York: Paulist, 1978), 59-78.

[8]*The Soul's Journey*, ch. 1:14.

[9]*The Soul's Journey*, chs. 3 and 4, esp. 3:1 and 3:5.

[10]This is the purpose of my dissertation. Cf. Calisi, "Bonaventure's Metaphysics of Self-diffusive Goodness and of Exemplarity as a Resource for Feminist Trinitarian Theology" (Ph.D. dissertation, Fordham University, 1997).

1. The primary thesis is to offer a sound theological foundation to interpret the Trinitarian names in an authentic, non-literal, non-patriarchal way.

2. If we ever do change or augment the Trinitarian formula in favor of gender-inclusive names, I offer Bonaventure's Trinitarian theology as a transitional phase, a bridge, to this change.

3. In my work in this area, I present Bonaventure's lavish use of gender-inclusive and gender-neutral names as a resource[11] for those with expertise in implementing them, especially in liturgy, the Eucharistic Canon, the Baptismal formula, the Creed, and in theological discourse. (The depth and breadth of these changes should make us seriously think about whether such a move would be wise.)

I developed the thesis of Bonaventure as a feminist resource because I saw that women were entering this exciting dialogue with diverse theological models of the Trinity. Elizabeth Johnson addresses the question from the theology of St. Thomas Aquinas.[12] Catherine LaCugna uses the theology of the Cappadocian Fathers (i.e., Sts. Basil, Gregory of Nyssa, and Gregory of Nazianzus).[13] And theologian Patricia Wilson-Kastner uses St. Augustine as her foundation for a feminist Trinitarian theology.[14] Bonaventure has much to offer this dialogue, and I base my thesis on his unique doctrine of the self-diffusive nature of the Good.

Briefly, this doctrine states that the good is self-diffusive.[15] Goodness must by nature diffuse itself, go out of itself, express itself, give of itself. God is absolute, perfect, infinite Goodness, and so God must by nature give of Godself, express Godself, absolutely,

---

[11]Calisi, 325 and 349.

[12]Elizabeth A. Johnson, *She Who Is: The Mystery of God in Feminist Theological Discourse* (New York: Crossroad, 1992).

[13]Cf. *God For Us* and "God in Communion With Us."

[14]Patricia Wilson-Kastner, *Faith, Feminism, and the Christ* (Philadelphia: Fortress, 1983), cf. ch. 6: "The Trinity."

[15]*The Soul's Journey*, 6:1 and 2. The principle of the self-diffusive good is from Pseudo-Dionysius. Cf. Pseudo-Dionysius, *The Celestial Hierarchy*, 4:1 and *The Divine Names*, 4:1 in *Pseudo-Dionysius: The Complete Works*, trans. Colm Luibheid, The Classics of Western Spirituality (New York: Paulist, 1987).

perfectly, and infinitely in generating the Son and spirating the Holy Spirit.

I would like to present briefly some background on the feminist critique of the traditional Trinitarian formula, and then I will discuss what Bonaventure has to offer.

Background for the Feminist Critique of the Trinitarian Formula

Feminist Christians have critiqued the exclusive use of male metaphors and images for God, arguing that it: 1) gives the impression that God is male, 2) depicts God as the single ruling male, the monarch, 3) perpetuates a literal understanding of the un-namable God, 4) leads to idolatry, 5) legitimates the hegemony of the ruling male human being in the form of a familial patriarch or a monarch, a king, or an emperor, and 6) supports and justifies patriarchal culture.

Patriarchy literally means the "rule of the father," and has come to mean the situation in which men dominate and/or are considered supreme on the sole basis of their gender. It is marked by an unequal treatment of women and by hierarchical relationships in which women are subordinated. Patriarchy believes that women are created for men (not men for women, nor both for mutuality), and that maleness is normative for what it means to be human, i.e., androcentrism.

Patriarchy is the system of male domination over women. The position of *paterfamilias*, the family patriarch, was in the past (and still is, to varying degrees in some cultures) one of almost absolute power over all members and property of his household. The members of the household included the wife or wives, concubines, children (including adult children and their spouses), servants, and slaves. The *paterfamilias* had the power to order or to forbid marriages or divorces, to sell or to give away any member of his household, to practice infanticide, and to murder offending house members. His sons could become heads of their own households someday. Men came to be associated with ownership of property, education, power, leadership, independence, and the public sphere.

Women were, in some sense, owned.[16] They were less educated, powerless, subjugated, and relegated to the domestic and private sphere.[17]

Feminism is the critique of patriarchy. Its purpose is nothing more and nothing less than actualizing the full humanity and therefore the full equality of women in theory and in practice, in every aspect of human existence. It is concerned with the well-being of women, however *they* define their own well-being. Feminism's moral grounding impels it to be concerned with the human dignity and well-being of men just as much as that of women. Men need to be liberated from the dehumanizing values and oppression of patriarchy as well. Feminist Christians critique patriarchy in all its manifestations in the Church and profoundly believe that it is contrary to God's intent.

It is indisputable that the names for God, including the Trinitarian names, have arisen out of a patriarchal culture, in which "man is the measure," i.e., maleness is definitive for every aspect of human existence (except procreation). Christianity most often uses male names for God and sometimes gender-neutral references as well (Creator, Word, Comforter), but never female names or feminine pronouns. No Christian seriously believes, on an intellectual level, that God is male. However, this may not be the case on an emotional or unconscious level, as evidenced in theological statements such as "God is not male, *He* is pure spirit." Often the conceptualization of God is not consciously one of a *man*, for such a concept would be dismissed as anthropomorphic by most thinking people. However, we cannot underestimate the power on the subconscious of the visual image of God as the male Caucasian octogenarian especially when coupled with its attendant verbal images of God the Father, Lord, King, and masculine pronouns.

---

[16]Even when women were not bought and sold as slaves, there were times (right into the twentieth century in the United States and England) in which women lacked their human and civil rights. The legal doctrine of *femme coverte* stated that a woman was covered under the law by the presence of a man (usually her father or husband). In short, a woman was considered a "legal minor" and had no right to vote, acquire an education, own property (her inheritance became her husband's upon marriage), or sign contracts. Her husband could legally beat her with a stick no wider than his thumb (i.e., "the rule of thumb"). She was a human being deprived of her right of self-determination.

[17]Sandra M. Schneiders, *Beyond Patching: Faith and Feminism in the Catholic Church* (New York: Paulist Press, 1991), 22.

Christian feminism exposes the idolatry which has been engendered by such an unconscious literalism. It makes us think seriously about what our metaphors and images really express about God, and it renews the orthodox Christian teaching about God's incomprehensibility and ineffability as Holy Mystery.

The feminist position is that because God is personal but transcends gender we may certainly refer to and address God with female metaphors, images, and pronouns. Women are created in one and the same divine image as men, and therefore female images and metaphors reflect God as well. Thus, feminists have retrieved female and gender-neutral images and metaphors from the Scriptures,[18] early Christian literature, early Christian wisdom Christologies,[19] the mystical tradition,[20] and women's experience.

A few examples of alternative names for God include: "Creator, Redeemer, Sustainer;" "Creator, Christ, Holy Spirit;" "Creator, Savior, Healer;" and "Source, Servant, Guide."[21] The ministers at Riverside Church in New York City baptize "in the name of the Father and of the Son and of the Holy Spirit, One God, Mother of us all;"[22] and the United Church of Christ baptizes in the traditional name of the Trinity, but balances the male metaphors with female metaphors in other parts of the baptismal liturgy. The "Prayer for the Baptized," for example, begins with "We give thanks, O Holy One, Mother and Father of all the faithful. . . ."[23]

---

[18]Some who oppose inclusive language for God make the distinction between metaphor and simile, arguing that there are no female metaphors for God in Scripture (there are similes), and that God is never addressed by a female name. Cf. Roland Frye, "Language for God and Feminist Language: Problems and Principles," in *Speaking the Christian God: The Holy Trinity and the Challenge of Feminism*, ed. Alvin F. Kimel (Grand Rapids, MI: Eerdmans Publishing Co., 1992), 17-43 and Garrett Green, "The Gender of God and the Theology of Metaphor," *Speaking the Christian God*, 44-64. They fail to note that Sophia in the Hebrew Scriptures is a metaphor, indeed She is divine Wisdom personified, a hypostasis.

[19]Cf. Elisabeth Schussler Fiorenza, *In Memory of Her: A Feminist Reconstruction of Christian Origins*, (New York: Crossroad, 1985), 132-135; Elizabeth A. Johnson, "Jesus, the Wisdom of God: A Biblical Basis for Non-androcentric Christology," *Ephemerides Theologicae Lovanienses*, LX 1:4 (1985): 261-294; Elizabeth A. Johnson, *She Who Is*.

[20]Cf. Caroline Walker Bynum, *Jesus as Mother: Studies in the Spirituality of High Middle Ages* (Berkeley, CA: University of California Press, 1982)

[21]Sharon Neufer Emswiler and Thomas Neufer Emswiler, *Women and Worship* (New York: Harper & Row, 1984), 93.

[22]Ruth C. Duck, *Gender and the Name of God: The Trinitarian Baptismal Formula* (New York: The Pilgrim Press, 1991), 163.

[23]United Church of Christ, *Book of Worship* (New York: United Church of Christ Office for Church Life and Leadership, 1986), 143.

The effort to uncover gender-inclusive metaphors and images in the tradition seems to have occurred in two overlapping stages. Initially, feminists rebelled against the image of God as the despotic male ruler, apart from a full reflection of the Trinity. Then, it became clearer that there was more at issue than dealing with names such as "Almighty Father." The father metaphor in Christianity invokes the whole Trinity; therefore, our conceptualization of God cannot be unitarian. What is at stake here is preserving the meaning of the revealed doctrine of the Trinity.

The course which this feminist theological investigation has taken reflects the Western Christian mentality of conceptualizing "the One God," of beginning with the Unity of God, and then of considering the triune God, i.e., the divine Persons. It is arguable that once feminist Christians addressed the question of the naming of the Persons, they discovered the divine relational nature to be contrary to the depiction of God as the unitary, male ruler of patriarchal culture. Once they considered the Trinitarian mystery as the mystery of God's relationality, it became clearer that Christ's disclosure of God was not of a solitary, unrelated and unrelatable Unmoved Mover and Ruler. In short, Trinitarian monotheism is more consistent and supportive of feminist values than unitarian monotheism. Authentic traditional teaching on the doctrine of the Trinity resonates with the feminist conceptualization of God.

I enter this feminist dialogue about the Trinitarian names of God with the assumption that male names in and of themselves need not be patriarchal. There are two levels of thought in understanding the doctrine of the Trinity. One is the immediate, superficial image that male images or metaphors evoke in the mind. The other is the deeper, underlying level of meaning that the images or metaphors mediate about incomprehensible Holy Mystery which will forever and eternally remain incomprehensible Holy Mystery.

Bonaventure's Doctrine of Self-diffusive Goodness and Feminist Trinitarian Theology

In his work, *The Soul's Journey into God*, Bonaventure begins a meditation on the names of God with God's own self-naming, as disclosed to Moses in the Hebrew Scriptures: "I Am Who Am" (Exod. 3:14).[24] For Bonaventure this is a revelation of the unity in God. He leads the reader in the contemplation of divine unity through God's name, Being. For Bonaventure, however, God's highest name is the Good,[25] for this is revealed in the New Testament in a verse in which Christ says, "No one is good but God alone" (Lk. 18:19 and Mt. 19:17). Goodness and love are convertible; of all things good, love is the best.[26] Therefore, the quotation from the First Letter of John, "God is love" (1 Jn. 4:8 and 16) is also relevant. In fact, in the absence of these "proof texts," it may be argued that the message that God is love and goodness is consistent with the spirit of the New Testament as a whole.

Bonaventure says that the good is self-diffusive. The nature of goodness *per se* is such that it must go out of itself; it must be fecund and productive, ecstatic and self-communicative, generous and self-expressive. Goodness is dynamic; it must act. It cannot merely "be."

Because God is eternal, infinite, and perfect, God must, by nature, communicate Godself in an eternal, infinite, and perfect way, withholding no quality from the Son. Because the Father communicates even the property of producing the Spirit, there is no subordination of the Son to the Father. And the Father and the Son, together as one principle, spirate the Holy Spirit, who is called their Love and Bond. Because God is essentially personal, divine self-expression produces an eternal communion of equal Persons in loving relationship.

God's essential goodness is the wellspring for the Second Person who is the Son. The word "Father," therefore, is a relational term which indicates that one Person comes forth from another. It is a relationship based on origin. Familial metaphors are the best

---

[24] *The Soul's Journey*, ch. 5.

[25] *The Soul's Journey*, 6:1 and 2.

[26] Cf. Richard of St. Victor: "We have learned above that in that supreme and altogether perfect good there is fullness and perfection of all goodness. However, where there is fullness of all goodness, true and supreme charity cannot be lacking. For nothing is better than charity; nothing is more perfect than charity. However, no one is properly said to have charity on the basis of his own private love of himself. And so it is necessary for love to be directed toward another for it to be charity. Therefore, where a plurality of persons is lacking, charity cannot exist." In *The Trinity*, Book 3, ch. 2, trans. Grover A. Zinn. The Classics of Western Spirituality (New York: Paulist Press, 1979).

expressions of how the divine Persons are related to each other because they are personal and intimate. They disclose the eternal origin of one Person from another, and it is precisely the eternal origin which distinguishes the Persons. This origin of Persons is eternal and "does not indicate priority in being, or time or eminence, but refers to the fact that God is absolutely personal."[27] The Father generates the Son because God is love, and an interpersonal relationship is necessary for the perfection of love. The Son is also called the Word and Image because the Son reflects all that the Father infinitely is and returns the Father's love as only an infinite Person can. This reciprocated Love is also a Person, the Holy Spirit acting as the Gift and Bond between them. This understanding of God is highly dynamic, ecstatic, and fecund.

This discussion on the inner life of God—however limited it may be—gives us an insight into God's "nature." This is not to say that we can know *what* God is, but we may know something about *how* God is. God's mode of being is to be relational. We know this to be true because we believe God has revealed Godself—as Father, Son, and Spirit—in the economy of salvation, and not something other than God. It is legitimate, therefore, to discuss God's inner life because God's inner life *is* God's life with us and vice versa.[28]

As stated earlier, we are really working on two levels. The first is the immediate level of simple "naming." The second level encompasses the various connotations and shades of meaning which the name mediates. Some of these connotations are intentional and salutary, some unintentional and pernicious. The naming of God as "Father" has the immediate effect of evoking certain mental and emotional images which may vary based on the individual subject's experience of "father" or which may evoke the well-known image of a male caucasian octogenarian. On the second, deeper level, the name of "Father" mediates important connotations such as loving relationality based on origin, goodness, and intimacy. Our problem with the way we name God seems to be that the metaphor which delivers these and other indispensable connotations also evokes a male image. However, if the metaphor "Father" is accorded a long

---

[27]*God For Us*, 245.

[28]This is Karl Rahner's axiom: "The 'economic' Trinity *is* the 'immanent' Trinity and vice-versa." In Karl Rahner, *The Trinity*, trans. Joseph Donceel (New York: Herder and Herder, 1970), 22. Emphasis by Rahner.

and thoughtful consideration, it becomes evident that even the fact that it is a male image is not really the problem. The problem is the use of male metaphors literally and patriarchically.

The invaluable elements of Bonaventure's unique way of understanding the triune God are critically correlated with Christian feminist theory so that the Trinity's essential meaning, God's Self-disclosure in the economy, may be extricated from its historically literal and patriarchal captivity. Bonaventure's model of the Trinity facilitates our understanding of the metaphors of "Father" and "Son" as a relationship based on origin, and it facilitates our understanding of God as tri-personal, infinitely good, essentially equal, absolutely loving, and dynamically self-emptying. As in many modern Trinitarian theologies, I accept the proposition that the structure of inner divine life may become a pattern to be reproduced among human beings.

Feminists who are Christians should not decline a Trinitarian theology in which God's depiction is such that the Father must, by nature and by necessity of being supreme goodness, empty Himself so fully, so infinitely, so unreservedly, in love in order to be fulfilled, in order to be God. Bonaventure's depiction of God the Father does not even remotely resemble the *paterfamilias* or a monarch in the modern sense of the word, nor any male ruling figure. Bonaventure presents the Father as Self-diffusive Goodness, Fecund Love, the *Fontalis Plenitudo* or the Fountain-fullness of divine life. These names do not indicate rule, dominance, self-sufficiency, or preeminence, but rather relationality, ecstatic communication, and the impetus to share Being. When Bonaventure begins his Trinitarian discourse with the Person of the Father, it is because he understands the Father's primacy as nothing other than the Father's kenotic, unifying, and inexhaustible fecundity.[29]

The image of the ruling male monarch is not consonant with Bonaventure's understanding of God's Fatherhood, primarily because he never gives even the slightest indication that he thinks it is a literal name. The name Father is not a proper name, but the relational term which connotes his principle of dynamic and personal origin within the Trinity. Secondarily, it is because

---

[29]*I Sent.*, d.2, a.1, q.2, fund. 4. and *I Sent.*, d.27, p.1, a.u., q.2, ad 3.

Bonaventure's Trinitarian theology is anchored in the economy (the touchstone for all metaphors) that the patriarchal figure is antithetical and repugnant to God's Self-revelation in Jesus Christ. Patriarchy and all forms of oppression are unequivocally antithetical to an authentic understanding of a Trinitarian God. As Catherine LaCugna states: "According to patriarchy, the male stands in relationship to everything and everyone else the way the nontrinitarian God is assumed to stand in relationship to the world."[30] The relationality of the tri-Personal God cannot be conceived in the way the patriarch relates to others.

> [A]ccording to the reign preached by Jesus Christ, patriarchy is not God's *arche*; [that is to say,] the rule of the male is not the rule of God."[31] . . . The strongest possible defense against sexism is . . . to argue ontologically . . . that the [very] *being* of God is utterly antithetical to every kind of subordination and subservience.[32]

The God of Jesus Christ is the Father of the prodigal son (Lk. 15:11-32); the one who knows how to give good things to all who ask (Mt. 7:11); who makes the sun rise on the evil and the good and sends rain on the just and the unjust (Mt. 5:43); who is the Font of life who raises Jesus from the dead and the Wellspring overflowing with mercy and justice.

It is unequivocally clear from the preceding discussion that the image of the *paterfamilias* has nothing to do with the Father of Jesus Christ. Fatherhood must be always understood in non-literal, non-patriarchal, non-idolatrous ways; the only authentic interpretation of the term "Father" is as an indication of intimacy, mutuality, and relationality based on origin. Therefore, God the Mother expresses equally well Christ's revelation of who and how God is within Godself and for us. LaCugna makes an argument that God's Motherhood is perhaps a better expression than God's Fatherhood:

> It should be evident by now that "Father" is not a literal term of biology. "Father" as much as "Mother" indicates Origin. In many respects Mother expresses much better

---

[30]*God For Us*, 393.
[31]*God For Us*, 394.
[32]*God For Us*, 287. Emphasis by LaCugna.

> than Father the utterly deep and . . . substantial . . . bond
> between God and creature, between source and offspring.
> Because the child literally comes forth from the Mother,
> the relationship between child and Mother is primary and
> more inherent or intrinsic than with the Father whose
> biological connection with the offspring simply cannot be
> the same.[33]

Moreover, it is by precisely the same logic that Daughter and Child, as much as Son, express the same intimacy, mutuality, and relationality based on origin for the pre-existent, immanent Logos.

The point, here, in discussing the Mother metaphor for God, is simply to shatter the idols of literalism and to remind us of the authentic Christian teaching of God's incomprehensibility. The use of many metaphors, images, and analogies for God aids in this. Bonaventure does not hesitate to use many names for God in his Trinitarian discourse. He calls the Parental Person *Fontalis Plenitudo* or Fountain Fullness, Fecund Source, Unoriginate Origin, Self-diffusing Goodness, Fecund Love, the Unbegotten One, *(innascibilistas)*, and Fontal-overflowing Source. For the Filial Person he offers Word, Wisdom, Exemplar, the *Persona Media* or the Central Person, and Perfect Image; and for the Pneumatic Person, Spirit, Gift, Bond, Love, Bond of Love, and Comforter. Such names enrich our theology, vivify our religious imagination, and allow us to speak about the ineffable rather than to remain silent. However, no name, metaphor, or image other than the familial metaphors—Father/Mother, Son/Child—convey the fact that God is both personal and relational, and that relationship is one based on origin.

Conclusion

The revelation of the Mystery of Trinity is the Mystery of God's life with us. It is a revelation about the meaning of personhood, of relationality, of self-emptying donation, and self-transcending love. Questions about equality, mutuality, roles, and non-subordination are part of the discourse on the Trinity, as they have been from the time of the Arian controversy. These questions are also part of the discourse on the human condition in the world.

---

[33]*God For Us*, 303.

Much can be quarried out of Bonaventure's work which is consonant with feminist values and concerns. Because of Bonaventure's philosophical principle of the self-diffusive good, his vision of the Holy Trinity is thoroughly permeated with superabundant, overflowing, interpersonal love. It approximates a "reason" for the existence of a plurality of Persons in God. His is a model of the Trinity which eschews an image of the Father wherein the values are self-possession, self-sufficiency, and isolation, arguably "the ultimate projection of masculinity."[34] Rather, his model is passionately involved with the personal and is exemplary of values indispensable to human community, i.e., equality, self-donation, and reciprocity.

In my dissertation,[35] I argue that Bonaventure is a good resource for a feminist reconstruction of Trinitarian theology for the following reasons:

- His model of the Trinity makes assertions about the triune God on the basis of the economy, i.e., drawn from God's self-revelation through Christ and in the Spirit;
- In this very economy God has freely communicated God*SELF*, and not something other than God, and this communication should be honored;
- His model flows out of fecund, fontal-overflowing goodness and love;
- His model is faithful to the revelation of relationality based on eternal *origin*;
- His model posits personhood, i.e., one oriented toward another, as the meaning of "Being;"
- His model presents interpersonal relations as exemplars of ecstatic, self-transcending, self-giving, interdependent, and mutual love;
- His model is by absolute necessity a communion of equal Persons;
- His model is of a God who comes to be Godself though the love of another;

---

[34]*God For Us*, 398.
[35]Calisi, 219-20.

- His model is exceedingly serious about the belief that human beings are created in the triune image;
- His model of inner divine life can be reflected by the bearers of the divine image in their capacity to know and to love in self-transcendence;
- The ultimate purpose of this kind of model is to reveal the life to which we are called and by which we are divinized, and thereby enter into the very life of God.

It would be a missed opportunity if Christians could not transcend the immediate level of the male names of Father and Son and arrive at the underlying level of meaning, which can be conveyed only by an intensely personal image of God, such as Bonaventure's Trinitarian image.

The next generation has an immeasurable and invaluable resource for theology in Franciscan studies. Bonaventure's principle of divine self-diffusion is just one example of how his work in particular, and Franciscan theology in general, can help us address profound theological questions in the modern world, while remaining faithful to truths revealed in the economy of salvation. It is an example of maintaining the tension between "continuity and development" in doing theology and of how we may ground modern theology, such as feminist theology, in the tradition.